In
MATERIAL
POSSESSIONS?

In Search of MATERIAL POSSESSIONS?

by Harold R. Dewberry, Ph.D., M.R.Ed.

Bridge-Logos

Gainesville, Florida 32614

In Search of Material Possessions?
by Harold R. Dewberry

Bridge-Logos

Gainesville, FL 32614 USA

Copyright ©2005 by Bridge-Logos

Printed in the United States of America.

Library of Congress Catalog Card Number: pending
International Standard Book Number 0-88270-804-X

Unless otherwise noted, all Scripture notations are taken from the New King James Version (NKJV) of the Bible.

Other Bible versions used include:
(RSV) Revised Standard Version
(WET) Wuest Expanded Translation
(TLB) The Living Bible
(AMP) The Amplified Bible

G163.316.m505.35240

Contents

Preface

The foundational material for this book comes from my taped series, *Stewardship*. The popularity of this series, and the encouraging feedback it generated led to putting these teachings in the form of a book. The inspiration that motivated this series of sermons came through a challenge by the Holy Spirit to find a scriptural balance in the area of stewardship. Many Christians do not seek true holiness of heart, self-worth and acceptance through a personal intimacy with the Lord, but instead seek a relationship with God by attaining monetary gain.

In an attempt to prove their faith and faithfulness, these Christians replaced godliness with contentment in their lives with the abundance of material possession and wealth (1 Timothy 6:9). However, instead of achieving godly piety with an inward sense of sufficiency in Christ, many find themselves devastated emotionally and experience grief and anxiety. As they seek to gain financial freedom, they find themselves in bondage to mountains of debt that refuse to be removed by positive thinking and confessions of faith.

The wholesome words of Jesus are substituted with doctrines that appeal to the basic instinct of self-preservation: pride and covetousness. Like Israel of old, which prospered under the reign of Jeroboam II, many put their faith and trust in provisions instead of the Provider. This leads to a false sense of spirituality and security. Money becomes much more than a tangible commodity when one's faith, affection and love are focused on it. Riches then grow into a living force and power to be equated with God, which in turn dethrones Christ from the center of the heart's affections.

The church in Laodicea was lukewarm, spiritually destitute, increased with goods and supposedly in need of nothing. However, the Spirit warned them, *"Behold, I stand at the door and knock"* (Revelation 3:20). This statement suggests that the Lord was positioned outside of their affections and no longer reigned at the center of their hearts.

Judas' love for power, which he exercised as holder of the moneybag, caused him to be divided in his loyalty. His love for mammon (riches) became greater than his love for God (Luke 16:13), so he sided with Christ's enemies, and reaped the reward for his iniquities:

> *He purchased a field with the reward of his iniquities (his love for unrighteous mammon) and having fallen flat on his face, he crashed open at the waist with a crashing noise and all of his inner organs gushed out. And it became known to all of the residents of Jerusalem, so that the piece of ground came to be called in their own language Akeldamach, that is, a bloody piece of ground, for it stands written in the Book of Psalms, let his place of abode become deserted, and let there not be he who establishes his permanent residence in it, and his office let another person of a different character take (Acts 1:18-20 WET).*

It's tragic when those gifted of God allow their desire for riches to be their motivation for service. Spiritual advancement in the Kingdom of God depends on one's proper handling of the money entrusted to them (Luke 16:11). For example, Barnabas, called the Son of Consolation, was commended for his selfless contribution (Acts 4:37). On the other hand, Sapphira and Ananias opened the doorway for

Satan to fill their hearts, and they lied to the Holy Spirit by their wrong attitude toward giving.

"And be not conformed to this world, but be transformed by the renewing of your mind, that you may prove what is that good and acceptable and perfect will of God" (Romans 12:2 NKJV).

This book attempts to set in order several key biblical teachings on wealth and prosperity that should be addressed by Christians of every age and station in life. It is my hope that by receiving this instruction, you will be set free from the distractions normally created by these issues and will be able to move into God's abundant provision.

However, be warned that much of what Scripture teaches about wealth (and our attitudes toward it) is contrary to popular secular and Christian notions. This book is not written to win the affection of its readers, but to call them into account with the truth. I believe that prayerful consideration of the points raised, together with the scriptural references presented, will result in increased blessing and release.

A Prophetic Warning

There is a tendency today to formulate our doctrine and interpretation of the Word of God to accommodate the subjective needs of society. Such interpretations obstruct the clear prophetic voice from being heard. The message is altered to adapt to today's values instead of addressing the need for repentance and a change of heart.

The primary danger in a time of financial crisis and recession is making an alliance with the world. Perhaps we don't realize that this weakens our faith and the power of the Gospel.

Isaiah warned Israel that its alliance with Egypt would be fruitless and that the real need was to rely on God (Isaiah 30). He portrayed the people loading their treasures on the backs of donkeys and the humps of camels, and tramping through the land of Negeb. Negeb represented a land of trouble and anguish—fertile ground for vipers and serpents, the lioness and lion. Despite Israel's efforts and precautions, Egypt's help proved worthless and empty.

This ancient prophecy of Isaiah warned God's people against union with the world's system—a word which appropriately applies to our day and time as well. When a worldwide recession is affecting all nations, the natural tendency is for the heart to be deceived into thinking that God will not discipline his people by the bread of adversity and the water of affliction.

We are standing at a crossroads. We can either:
• preach more about prosperity and accumulating material possession, or
• over-emphasize the denial of material provisions and become almost Gnostic in our spirituality.

Be careful of doctrines that promise prosperity by your own efforts and not by repentance of heart. Any doctrine that promises blessing without repentance is a false doctrine preached by those devoid of real spiritual insight (1 Timothy 6). But the Lord is gracious and full of mercy and patiently waits for His people to turn to Him.

In returning and rest you shall be saved; in quietness and in trust shall be your strength. Therefore the LORD waits to be gracious to you; therefore he exalts himself to show mercy to you (Isaiah 30:15,18 RSV).

We are in danger of polarizing some elements of truth that worked effectively because of our obedience to the Holy

Spirit's prompting. For instance, I'm sure there are those who have been healed as a result of sowing seed-faith money into someone's ministry. However, it's dangerous to make this a doctrine for all to follow. When Jesus sent out the twelve, He charged them:

> *"And preach as you go, saying, 'The kingdom of heaven is at hand. Heal the sick, raise the dead, cleanse lepers, cast out demons. You received without paying, give without pay'"* *(Matthew 10:7-8 RSV).*

Jesus activated faith and made it alive in other ways, as well. The Scripture gives examples of simple requests that demanded direct obedience to Him and not to the Law of Moses:

- Go wash...!
- Stretch forth...!
- Go show...!
- Raise up...!
- Take up...!

The physical result of obedience is not what is important, but the act of obedience itself...for the blessed man is one who hears and obeys (James 1:22-25).

Some have preached that faith is the way to financial freedom. Although we must agree that faith is an important element in our Christian walk, it is not greater than hope or love.

> *"Love which is the outward expression of humility of heart toward others is far greater than either hope or faith"* *(1 Corinthians 13:13 WET).*

Developing humility and the fear of the Lord opens the doorway for Christ to entrust us with the wealth of the world.

Perhaps it will be easier to comprehend this truth by examining these facts. At the very outset of human existence, the enemy of man's soul tempted him to disobey the Lord's commands with a subtle appeal to participate in worldly desires. Today the strategy is the same. We are enticed to indulge in our wants:

"... the craze for sex, the ambition to buy everything that appeals to you, and the pride that comes from wealth and importance" (1 John 2:16 TLB).

Because of Adam's disobedience, the Lord placed a curse upon the soil. God told Adam, *"I have placed a curse upon the soil. All your life you will struggle to extract a living from it"* (Genesis 3:17 TLB). Only when there is a full manifestation of the sons of God will the earth be set free:

For all creation is waiting patiently and hopefully for that future day when God will resurrect his children. For on that day thorns and thistles, sin, death, and decay—the things that overcame the world against its will at God's command—will all dIsaiahppear..." (Romans 8:19-21 TLB)

Profound truth is found in the concept of a grain of wheat falling into the ground and dying. When we lose our love for this world and everything it embraces, our soul is set free from selfishness and we are restored to function in the divinely appointed order. Then, and only then, will we achieve our full potential in this earthly life.

Self-worth is not gained by self-assertiveness. It's achieved through a relationship with the Lord Jesus. He restores us to a place of esteem because we have received the Spirit of Adoption or Sonship. Then we are restored to a right relationship with our heavenly Father. As we honor and highly esteem Christ, the Father esteems us. The Father honors us by being attentive to us, answering our prayers and meeting our needs (John 12:26, Romans 8:15-17).

Therefore, we have no need to be anxious about the things of the world: "what we should eat; what we should wear; what we should drink." As we place Christ in the right perspective in our lives, these material things are given to us to enjoy and share (Matthew 6:33-34). Then, we can be like Paul—content. Whether we have much or little, we are sufficient through Christ's sufficiency (Philippians 4:17 AMP). The world around us will share in the glorious freedom enjoyed by God's children. The things of nature, animals and plants, also suffer in sickness and death as they await this great release from the effects of sin on the world (Romans 8:19-23 TLB).

Very little is preached on the covenant that God made with Noah. This is called the Noahic Covenant or the Dispensation of Human Government (Genesis 8:21-23; 9:1-28). This covenant is eternal in concept; for the Lord will never again smite every living thing as He had previously done (verse 21). But with the giving of any covenant, there will also be a test of man's response.

> *Noah planted a vineyard; And he drank of the wine, and was drunken; and he was uncovered within his tent. And Ham, the father of Canaan, saw the nakedness of his father, and told his two brethren without. ... And Noah awoke from his wine, and knew what his younger son had done unto him. And he said, "Cursed be Canaan; a servant of servants shall he be unto his brethren" (Genesis 9: 20-21, 24-25).*

It is very hard to understand why Noah would place a curse on his grandson except when we study the word "naked." The word used here in the Hebrew text is different that the work *e-rom*, which is simply translated as "nakedness" or "nudity" (Genesis 2: 25). The word "naked" that is used in Genesis 3: 11 and Genesis 9: 22 is the word *e'wah*, which is the root Hebrew word for "shame." As we study the effect of shame, we see tat shame brings us under financial bondage.

The meaning of the word "Canaan" or "Cannaanite" is "to become in bondage financially to someone else." It means to be brought low by trafficking in money, to make wrong business decisions, to not have enough, and to suffer embarrassment because we lack financially.

Shame from a New Testament perspective is a loss of inner beauty, a disfigurement of personality. It is a false humility, a sense of worthlessness that keeps one in bondage to that which causes one to devalue self (2 Peter 2: 19b, AMP). To be released from the feelings of shame is one of the major keys to gaining material possessions.

Common Grace

Any discussion of wealth and provision must have its reference point in God Himself. The amazing truth is that God's gift of life entitles us to be the recipients of His generous giving and abundance.

Contrary to the notions subscribed to by our society and the endless barrage of misinformation we receive, we are fabulously wealthy because of the generosity of a living and eternal God. It seems almost childish to speak of such things, yet the revelation of our true state should be pondered by the most astute and mature minds.

God gives to His creation very generously. Life itself is an incalculable gift. The natural creation around us is a package of beauty and wonder at which every generation marvels. The variety of animals and plants, the wealth of resources and the abilities of man are all gifts from God.

We are rich beyond measure through one thing alone—life. At the moment of birth, you received this gift. Your minutes and days, your senses, your mind, your emotions, a world to perceive and fellow humanity to share it with are all priceless.

Every living soul is given all this wealth, at least for a time, without charge and without obligation.

None of these gifts were given out of any obligation on God's part. He owed us nothing, neither did we have any hold over Him to force Him to create excellently or provide us with anything beautiful or satisfying. The fact that we have anything at all is testimony to God's immeasurable goodness. He gives with an open heart and an open hand. So wonderful is God's heart toward us to bless us, that He gives good things to the just and the unjust alike. The following Scripture describes for us the perfection of God's character:

> *I say to you, love your enemies, bless those who curse you, do good to those who hate you, and pray for those who spitefully use you and persecute you, that you may be sons of your Father in heaven; for He makes His sun rise on the evil and on the good, and sends rain on the just and on the unjust. For if you love those who love you, what reward have you? Do not even the tax collectors do the same? And if you greet your brethren only, what do you do more than others? Do not even the tax collectors do so? Therefore you shall be perfect, **just as your Father in heaven is perfect** (Matthew 5:44-48* NKJV *emphasis added).*

The abundant provision poured out generously and without favor by God upon the just and the unjust is theologically entitled "Common Grace." We have all been partakers of this grace, and as Jesus taught in Matthew 5, we are to bestow this common grace upon others in the same manner extended to us by our Father in heaven.

Human Discontent

Many Christians are quick to complain about unpleasant or difficult situations in life and freely express to others everything they don't like about it. But, they are almost always silent when it comes to thanking God for the abundant free gift of life.

Sadly, we are far more aware of what we find lacking than what is ours in abundance. The flesh nature is geared toward satisfying its wants instead of appreciating and enjoying the things we have. The apostle John declared that the world is focused on lust and pride:

> "For all that is in the world—the lust of the flesh, the lust of the eyes, and the pride of life—is not of the Father but is of the world" (1 John 2:16 emphasis added).

This is why Paul so boldly declared that a person with contentment has attained great gain.

> "But godliness with contentment is great gain" (1 Timothy 6:6).

It is not normal for a person in this world to arrive at a place of contentment. For this reason, we easily despise the circumstances of our lives and ignore the fact that we are truly wealthy. God's people should be outstanding because they are filled with contentment instead of consumed with lust. They should always have a thankful attitude toward God, because thanksgiving is a fundamental element of the Christian experience:

> ...in everything **give thanks;** for this is the will of God in Christ Jesus concerning you. (1 Thessalonians 5:18 emphasis added)

> ...in everything by prayer and supplication, with **thanksgiving,** let your requests be made known to God. (Philippians 4:6 emphasis added)

Extra Grace on Some

This common grace has a disproportionate aspect. Some people are born into poverty and squalor in underdeveloped nations. They lack proper education, and their resources are undeveloped.

Others are born into highly developed cultures with an abundance of resources, which are often taken for granted. Theirs is a dangerous situation, as they operate under the assumption that privilege and abundance are theirs by some special right or personal accomplishment.

> You are not more blessed because you are more special.

Those of us living in highly developed societies with great technological, social and material wealth must realize two important things. First, privilege of birth does not make us superior people. Second, privilege does not suggest selective worthiness or special favor from God.

People born in underprivileged, deprived families or groups of people (i.e., a nation devastated by war and famine) fighting for daily basic survival are equally loved by the Living God as those of means. They are worthy of respect and eligible for eternal salvation to the same degree as the person born into a wealthy and influential family or highly developed society.

The facts that we have supermarkets bursting with great variety, educational systems that are highly developed, and a stable, democratic, national government do not establish worthiness in the eyes of God. These are all expressions of God's grace.

You are not more blessed because you are more special. Neither are you more blessed because you are more deserving. God in His grace allowed you to be born into one culture while another person was born at the opposite end of the spectrum.

So how should we respond to God's blessings and grace? How should we handle this incredible privilege of birth? Scripture says to handle it with thanksgiving.
And let the peace of God rule in your hearts, to which also you were called in one body; and be thankful.
(Colossians 3:15 emphasis added)

We should not compare our lives and respond with disapproval of those who have more of this world's goods. Consider the wondrous wealth and privilege we were given at birth compared to the millions born into oppression, lack, ignorance and darkness. Be thankful!

We must also heed the warning of Jesus: that servants are expected to be good stewards of whatever their master has entrusted to them. If servants abuse the privileges of their provision, they will face judgment. Jesus declared:
"For everyone to whom much is given, from him much will be required; and to whom much has been committed, of him they will ask the more" (Luke 12:48).

Having been born into great wealth and provision, we are under a great weight of responsibility. We cannot be compared to those who will die of starvation in childhood or to those who will never have an education, personal liberty or religious freedom. Much will be required of us, and the judgment upon what we do with our resources will be much more serious than upon those born with practically nothing.

The Treasure of Salvation

We have established that everyone shares equal blessing merely by living in a world created for him or her by God. However, the Christian is blessed with even greater riches that are far more wonderful than any natural treasure.

• Who can place a monetary value (or price tag) on forgiveness, peace, love or joy?

• How can the on-going wealth of God's Holy Spirit being our comforter and guide be calculated? How could we ever determine the full value of the truths freely given to us in God's word?

• How can the value of eternal life as God's children be established?

Again we must realize that God is under no obligation to give us such incomprehensible blessings. God does so because it's His desire to bless. God's love for us moves Him to give immeasurable blessings to an undeserving people. We are under the care of a God who is forever pouring out blessings!

Christians are in the family of an eternal God whose generosity is unfathomable. The foundational reality through which we can understand provision and blessing is this: God was generous beyond imagination before we existed and before we ever considered seeking or acquiring anything for ourselves.

Paul summed up God's generosity:
> *"He who did not spare His own Son, but delivered Him up for us all, how shall He not with Him also freely give us all things?"* *(Romans 8:32).*

Jesus declared, *"God so loved the world that He gave His only begotten Son"* (John 3:16), revealing that God's love demands that He be a giving God.

Is God a Depriver?

Most people don't start at the basic reference point when attempting to understand God as the great and generous giver of precious gifts. Sadly, people often believe that God deprives them of good things and must literally be forced into blessing them. Perhaps they feel miserable and undone because they lack a large collection of man-made gadgets and finery. They completely ignore or take for granted the more valuable things freely given without charge, and without them having to ask or strive for them.

Perhaps right now you can identify a number of things on your "wish list." There are probably at least a few things for which you have prayed but have not received. Or you may be aware of several things belonging to others that you'd like to have added to your list of possessions. But if you are to have a clear picture of God's plan for blessing your life, you must first see beyond the things you want. You must start with a revelation of truth and reality.

> You have already started life fabulously wealthy.

Therefore, let's begin our examination of wealth and possessions with this important realization: You have already started life fabulously wealthy. You are blessed beyond measure with things you did not earn, do not deserve and did not have to pay for. Think about it. All of those things are ample evidence of the generosity of God.

Give Thanks To God

Before reading any further, pause right now and give thanks to God. Thank Him for life itself, the greatest gift and privilege that He has given you. Thank God for the rich and beautiful creation He made for you to enjoy. Thank God for the salvation and spiritual blessings He's provided and poured out upon you. Thank God for loving you and wanting the best for you. Thank God for all of His thoughts toward you, thoughts for good and not for evil, to give you hope for a future (Jeremiah 29:11). Thank God that His plans for your life are far more wonderful than anything you could ever imagine for yourself. Finally, thank God for the greatest blessing of all—everlasting life in His presence in a world filled with incorruptible beauty and riches, a world with no more pain, sickness, grief or loss.

By giving thanks to God, you establish your relationship with Him on the facts that He is good and that He has already given good and perfect gifts to you and to all humanity. Break away from any notion that God is ill -tempered or vindictive and must be forced into giving good things. Recognize that God is the One who gives life, together with every perfect gift.

Now you can approach Him in faith and expectancy as you work through the following chapters of this book. The Lord blesses you as you encounter His truth.

– 2 –

The Wonder of Inheritance

Not only do we come into this life with a basket full of blessings from God's common grace and His salvation so freely given, but God also allows us to tap into an even greater abundance. He established the principle of inheritance that allows us to gain even more of His blessings and provisions. We can better understand the wonder of this inheritance when we consider what was provided for the Israelites. They were given an inheritance filled with blessings that they didn't deserve and could not possibly achieve for themselves. It was beyond all they could ask or think.

The promised inheritance for Israel included a land described as "flowing with milk and honey" (Exodus 3:8). The Israelites did not earn the inheritance or have any natural claim to the land and the accompanying blessings. But as God's chosen people, the Israelites received an inheritance established for them by God. He provided them with land for their very own use, together with promises of great prosperity, protection and security. Abundance was built into the inheritance, and it was this inheritance that set them apart from all other peoples and nations on the earth.

Notice that this new level of wonderful provision from God came in the form of grace. The inheritance was promised to Israel with no work required to attain it or special worthiness in and of themselves to deserve it. God chose Abraham from among the nations and conferred upon him the blessing of an inheritance for his generations. This is similar to the common grace already discussed. God does not owe it, but instead chooses to give.

The exciting aspect of this inheritance is that it provided the Israelites with a treasure to enjoy that they otherwise would have missed. Inheritance gave them something to look forward to, something to claim as their own, and it set them apart from the other nations. Inheritance gave them a hope for a future as a people. It was an entirely new parcel of wealth allotted by God to be enjoyed.

Christians are also provided with an inheritance. We are described as heirs as follows:
> "... *heirs of God and joint heirs with Christ" (Romans 8:17).*
> "... *if you are Christ's, then you are Abraham's seed, and heirs according to the promise" (Galatians 3:29).*
> "... *you are no longer a slave but a son, and if a son, then an heir of God through Christ" (Galatians 4:7).*

The Old Testament notion of inheritance was not limited to the material blessings conferred upon the nation of Israel. It also included spiritual blessings, now made available to God's children through faith in Jesus Christ (Galatians 3:29.). Therefore, inheritance is a principle that God established to confer special blessing upon His people, in the times of both the Old Testament and New Testament.

How to Inherit God's Best

Jesus taught us in His Sermon on the Mount how to inherit God's best. This principle of inheritance opens up a new realm of special blessings available for us. All of humanity can enjoy God's provision through the gift of life. However, as Christians we can inherit even greater abundance.

Jesus taught about several "blessed attitudes" that bring wonderful consequences (Matthew 5:3-12). These Beatitudes could well be called "Christ's laws of possession" because they teach us how to receive expanded provisions. Among the verses on this subject, we find teachings about how to take possession of the Kingdom of God and how to inherit the earth. Therefore, we have access by birth to the created blessings God provided and access by salvation to the spiritual blessings Christ purchased for us. But we also gain access to greater spiritual and temporal provision by following Jesus' teachings. We will now closely examine the keys to these two teachings.

Inheriting the Earth

> *"Blessed are the meek, for they shall inherit the earth"*
> *(Matthew 5:5).*

This is the key to taking possession of the world and its natural assets. It's important to have the proper attitude about this subject. We can possess but must hold lightly onto worldly and natural assets. They must not possess us, thereby weakening our loyalty and faith in God. We can be more than mere passengers on the earth, because we can lay claim to an inheritance from the earth and its resources.

Meekness is how to lay claim to an inheritance from the earth and its resources. Meekness is a somewhat vague and

11

an unappreciated quality today. It is often related to a mild-mannered weakness or wimpy attitude. The Greek word translated as "meek" in English paints quite a different picture. This word was used to describe the Roman war-horses going into battle. A horse worthy of being called meek was mighty, powerful and fearless. Yet, it was so highly trained and so yielded to the control of its rider that the slightest signal brought an immediate response.

Meekness is not the mistaken idea of wimpishness, but is power and might. For the horse this comes only through total surrender to its lord and master and quick response to the slightest impulse and lightest signal. Remember, God called Moses the meekest man on earth, and he was the man God chose to lead Israel into the Promised Land.

Is it any wonder that most people never inherit anything of this world's wealth? Perhaps the largest percentage of all people today is living in a form of "survival" mode. In third-world countries, people live from meal to meal. The majority of the population living in highly developed nations with a higher standard of living exists from paycheck to paycheck. The relative standard of living is higher, but the process and the reality are the same. They have not inherited the earth.

We fail to inherit the earth, because we've failed to develop meekness. Our culture worships self-indulgence instead of honoring and promoting meekness. We are not totally surrendered to the will of God and are not submitted to His discipline to the point of responding immediately to His slightest prompting. We may give God "lip service" by saying all the right things, but our hearts are far from Him. Self-indulgence is so deeply entrenched in our society that sales trainers have taught their students for decades that the basic question in the minds of Westerners is, "What's in it for me?"

The absurdity of the situation is that the consuming passion of most people is to "make good" and accumulate as much of this world's goods as possible for their own selfish purposes. Yet in this, they miss the very thing they seek. The intent of their hearts is misplaced and the wrong motivations drive them to vainly pursue empty values. They don't develop meekness so they cannot inherit what they so desperately long to possess.

There is a great difference between those who inherit the earth and those with limited access to its resources. Most of us see the world as belonging to someone else. We consider the wealthy, the landowners, the industrialists and the like as the owners of the earth's riches and resources. The most common opinion is the capitalists own the earth and the workers have to take it back from them. Even in a capitalistic society, we believe our purpose in life is to work to gain as much as possible of the earth and its goods for ourselves. But this idea betrays us in that we fail to see ourselves as inheritors of the earth.

> There is a great difference between those who inherit the earth and those with limited access to its resources.

Heirs don't have to fight for what rightfully belongs to them. They do not have to pit themselves in a struggle against others to possess what is theirs by inheritance. Yet the world system today generates the constant battle to gain something from the earth and from those who supposedly own its wealth. The ambitious trample over anyone who gets in the way, leaving the broken and wounded strewn in every direction. As the saying goes, "It's a dog-eat-dog world."

Practical Meekness

What exactly do we mean by practical meekness? Practical meekness is bringing one's life under control in order to meaningfully submit to God.

Many come to God intending to fully yield their lives to Him, but in reality, they yield only a portion. The rest is not under control. They make promises to stop swearing, clean up their thoughts, habits or life-style, but are unable to deliver on those promises.

Why is this? The answer is that these people exercise no control over their tongues, thoughts, habits or life-styles. The truth is that self-indulgence has brought about an abdication of the will as the ruler over their lives. They are slaves to the lusts of the flesh and the pride of life. Therefore, they have set themselves up for a war to the death with the flesh in order to become the person God intends them to be. That's why Paul teaches: *"Those who are Christ's have crucified the flesh with its passions and desires" (Galatians 5:24).*

Meekness is a state of being wherein our natural affections and lusts are brought under submission to the Spirit. In fact, the control is so complete that no matter what God requests we are willing and able to perform it. No complaint or reaction from within will have power to interfere with our obedience.

It must be noted here that if people had the ability to completely deal with their human nature, they would not need Christ. Keep in mind that our human nature was corrupted when Adam disobeyed God in the Garden of Eden and that Christ's redemption is appropriated through our obedience. We do not have the power within ourselves to do what is good and to cease from doing what is bad. We need

God's help. That is why Paul also taught that, *"if **by the Spirit** you put to death the deeds of the body, you will live"* (Romans 8:13). God is the ultimate power to deal with our flesh (human nature), but we must be intent on achieving that total yielding by allowing Him to develop meekness in our lives.

Many things reveal the lack of meekness, including anger, uncontrolled responses, the inability to keep our word, and making excuses for our inappropriate actions.

The moment you surrender to any natural impulse in your life, you disqualify yourself from inheriting the earth. You can't lay claim to the riches of this earth if you are given to:
- Anger
- Resentment
- Frustration
- Intolerance
- Indulgence
- Quickness of tongue
- Inconsistency
- Unfaithfulness
- Shallowness
- Self-justification
- Any evidence of unrestraint

This is not to suggest that we must embark on a program of rigorous holiness through our own power of will. As stated earlier, freedom must come "by the Spirit" (Romans 8:13). Our weaknesses, vulnerabilities and the lack of meekness can't be changed by an act of our will. Will power is not our savior. God is our Savior, through Jesus Christ and the power of the Holy Spirit.

Meekness is listed as a fruit of the Spirit in Galatians 5:23. Meekness is not achieved by the use of our fleshly resources, but only by yielding to the power of the Holy Spirit. Meekness should be a natural outcome of submission to the Lord and not a naturally developed skill or discipline.

Possessing the Kingdom of Heaven

According to the teachings of Jesus, we are not only able to inherit the earth, but we are also to possess the Kingdom of God. Jesus said twice in the Beatitudes that we could have the kingdom of heaven, and He taught two ways of achieving it:

> 1. *"Blessed are the poor in spirit, for theirs is the kingdom of heaven"* (Matthew 5:3).
> 2. *"Blessed are those who are persecuted for righteousness sake, for theirs is the kingdom of heaven"* (Matthew 5:10).

What does it mean to possess the kingdom of heaven?

Possessing the kingdom possibly suggests different ideas to different people. Many people assume that it refers to having a place in heaven when we die. This is true, of course, but I believe it has a far more significant and wonderful meaning than that.

Jesus began His earthly ministry with a sermon that was a call to *"Repent, for the kingdom of heaven is at hand"* (Matthew 4:17). He then spent three years in ministry demonstrating in dramatic and practical ways the reality of having the kingdom of heaven at hand. The full meaning of having the kingdom of heaven is found in what Jesus did. He:
- healed lepers
- opened blind eyes
- cast out demons
- raised the dead

- miraculously fed the multitudes
- taught life-changing truths
- defeated the devil
- forgave sins
- cured all manner of sicknesses
- released the tormented
- called people into powerful new lives
- brought hope and joy where there was only defeat and death

The kingdom of heaven is not only a future blessing awaiting us after death, but something that is at hand. It is the power of heaven brought into our daily lives, so that which is not achievable by natural means occurs supernaturally in our lives. The kingdom of heaven is bringing the eternal and spiritual realities to bear on natural situations, generating results that a natural man can't acquire by any natural means. It is the ability to live with heaven's resources being manifested upon the earth's territory. To possess the kingdom of heaven here on earth is a most wonderful blessing. It is a blessing that should be taken seriously and sought after with single-minded determination.

Consider the value of having God's power resident within to resolve all the medical problems of your family throughout your life. What about the value of having God's mind on every situation you face and every decision you must make?

How do you put value on the power to overturn every ploy of the devil? Possessing the kingdom of heaven is in itself a great source of wealth. Those who possess it are far richer than those who possess the more visible types of wealth and riches. After all, *the things that are seen are only temporary, but the things that are unseen are eternal* (2 Corinthians 4:18).

How can we estimate the value of peace? Multitudes of people, with an abundance of material possessions, have, in a sense, killed themselves because they've lost their inner peace.

How do we put a dollar value on forgiveness? Multitudes have lived tormented lives, despite their amassed possessions, simply for want of feeling forgiven and clean again.

Ask anyone tormented by demonic voices or madness of any sort how much they would give to be free. Ask those with incurable diseases what full health is worth to them. The blessings of the kingdom of heaven are in themselves wealth that can't be calculated.

How do we possess the kingdom of heaven? Jesus taught that the kingdom of Heaven is ours by becoming "poor in spirit" and being totally committed to righteousness. However, this commitment means being willing to endure persecution for the sake of righteousness.

Poor in Spirit

To be poor in spirit simply means we don't consider ourselves having resources of our own within our own person. We declare ourselves poor in natural and spiritual resources and do not rely on or boast about our own knowledge and abilities. Jesus was the perfect example of this in His earthly ministry. Despite the fact that Jesus is the Son of God, He never did anything of Himself. He acted and spoke only as the Father prompted Him. He made Himself poor in spirit and depended totally on God. He did not rely upon His own immeasurable resources.

> *The Son can do nothing of Himself but what He sees the Father do; for whatever He does, the Son also does*

18

in like manner ... I can of myself do nothing. As I hear, I judge, and my judge, and my judgment is righteous, because I seek not my own will but the will of the Father who sent Me ... But that the world may know that I love the Father, and as the Father gave Me commandment, so I do. (John 5:19, 30, 14:31)

The kingdom of heaven is for the righteous and there is ample Scripture to confirm that no unrighteous person will enter heaven:

...unless your righteousness exceeds the righteousness of the Scribes and Pharisees, you will by no means enter the kingdom of heaven (Matthew 5:20).

Do you not know that the unrighteous will not inherit the kingdom of God? (1 Corinthians 6:9)

For this you know, that no fornicator, unclean person, nor covetous man, who is an idolater, has any inheritance in the kingdom of Christ and God. (Ephesians 5:5)

But there shall by no means enter into it anything that defiles, or causes an abomination or a lie, but only those who are written in the Lamb's Book of Life. (Revelation 21:27)

Those who wish to see and possess the Kingdom of Heaven here on earth should stand for righteousness so clearly and distinctly that the unrighteous persecute them.

In this generation, we have strongly tried to avoid persecution. We are bluffed into thinking that, since we live in a Christian community and a nation with Christian values, we can live in peace and harmony free from persecution. But this idea is not taught in Scripture. The Bible teaches that Christians have an inner peace, but *"all who desire to live godly in Christ Jesus will suffer persecution"* (2 Timothy 3:12).

People persecuted for the sake of righteousness are not radical extremists. They are simple Christians who stand for Christ's principles.

Persecution is mentioned in connection with living godly in Christ Jesus because you will never really know how committed you are to anything until you take a firm stand for it in the midst of persecution. If you shrink before persecution, ridicule, betrayal, a challenge to your faith or similar circumstances, you've robbed yourself of the blessing of possessing the kingdom of heaven. You will never know the matchless power of God's presence, guidance, protection, provision and miracles made available in such times as these.

Two Principles of Possession

These simple teachings of Jesus point to two key principles for wealth and possessions.

1. To inherit the earth and enjoy the things God created for us, we must have our natural life in control and under submission to the Lordship of Christ. If we do not bring our natural life under His control, then God will not give us control over this natural world. Therefore, meekness is required.

2. To possess and enjoy the eternal, spiritual things God has prepared for us, we must have our spiritual life in control and submission. If we do not submit our spiritual life to God's control, then we will not have access to the spiritual kingdom prepared for us. Being "poor in spirit" is an attitude. It refuses to rely on self or any outside source other than God for

fulfillment, meaning, purpose, blessing, salvation, righteousness or whatever.

The above principles could be expressed in these specific ways:
- Indulge in lusts and you end up empty and destitute of natural blessings.
- Indulge in the pride of your own ability and you end up empty and destitute of spiritual blessing.

Jesus' Example

While on the cross, Jesus was the perfect picture of meekness, poverty of spirit and enduring persecution for righteousness' sake.

Jesus brought under control His natural urge for self-preservation, revenge, personal defense, comfort, escape from pain and all the other ugly natural human inclinations. Jesus ruled His own spirit and did not give in to those temptations. Facing great pressure and personal desire to avoid the situation, with all the might and power of heaven at His disposal, Jesus meekly walked the deadly path God had set for Him. He ignored the taunts, allowed the beatings and people spitting in His face, and headed purposefully toward the brutality He was to bear on the cross. Then, after everything the people had put Him through, He gave them full and free forgiveness, although not one of them was asking for it. This is the glory of meekness.

Jesus remained poor in spirit during every event of that terrible day. Jesus did not assume that He could take over the process, nor did He allow His own perceptions, reactions or assessments to influence Him. Jesus revealed His strong personal wish to avoid the crucifixion while praying in the

21

Garden of Gethsemane. Nevertheless, His own spirit remained poor, and He did not exalt His interests above those of God's:

> *"He went a little farther and fell on His face, and prayed, saying, 'O my Father, if it be possible, let this cup pass from me: nevertheless not as I will, but as you will'"* *(Matthew 26:39).*

There is no shortage of evidence that Jesus was persecuted for righteousness' sake. Jesus was not crucified because He had done anyone wrong by killing, stealing, cheating or hurting them. Despite Jesus' righteousness, He was crucified because His stand incensed and outraged those who loved the darkness. Consider this: persecution of the righteous exposes to the world the ugliness and total depravity of evil, which cannot coexist with that which is pure and holy. Therefore, evil is compelled by its very nature to destroy everything that is godly.

Jesus was meek, poor in spirit and persecuted for righteousness. According to His own teaching, He should have possessed both the earth and heaven. And He did:

> *...who, being in the form of God, did not consider it robbery to be equal with God, but made Himself of no reputation, taking the form of a bondservant, and coming in the likeness of men. And being found in appearance as a man, He humbled Himself and became obedient to the point of death, even the death of the cross. Therefore God also has highly exalted Him and given Him the name which is above every name, that at the name of Jesus every knee should bow, of those in heaven, and of those on earth, and of those under the earth, and that every tongue should confess that Jesus Christ is* LORD, *to the glory of God the Father (Philippians 2:6-11).*

Jesus was God and thought it not robbery to be equal with God, but He put all that aside and became of no reputation. In other words, He became poor in spirit. Jesus ceased to rely upon Himself with His own rights and privileges as equal with God, but submitted Himself to God the Father. In becoming a man, Jesus took upon Himself the form of a servant and was obedient even to death on the cross. To be completely obedient, Jesus suffered by bringing His human instincts and impulses under total control, which is meekness.

We know from Hebrews 5:8 that Jesus' obedience involved the suffering of bringing His life under control in order to fulfill what was expected of Him. That suffering was also persecution for righteousness' sake.

In return for Jesus' meekness and poverty of spirit, He was given a Name above every name, to which everything must bow, both in heaven (possessing the kingdom of heaven) and in earth (inheriting the earth).

Jesus is the inheritor of all things:

> God, who at various times and in various ways spoke in time past to the fathers by the prophets, has in these last days spoken to us by His Son, whom He has appointed heir of all things, through whom also He made the worlds (Hebrews 1:1-2).

Jesus is the proof of His own teaching that we can have much more than the blessings provided at birth or the blessings of salvation. If we would only develop the character that Jesus taught and exemplified in His own life, we could be the rightful possessors of this world and of God's Kingdom.

An Overlooked Prosperity

There is still another form of prosperity completely ignored today but covered in the Beatitudes. That is, the domain of personal relationships: *"Blessed are the merciful, for they shall obtain mercy"* (Matthew 5:7).

It is one thing to inherit the earth and have this natural world yielding its fruit to us. It is quite another thing to possess the kingdom of heaven with heavenly and supernatural blessings enriching our lives. Money and spiritual gifts do not guarantee harmony with our friends or our family. To receive the riches of good personal relationships, we must be willing to make an investment. We must show mercy to receive mercy.

This truth about making investments in people to receive the benefit of good social wealth is amplified in these verses as well:

> *Judge not, that you be not judged. For with what judgment you judge, you will be judged; and with the measure you use, it will be measured back to you (Matthew 7:1-2).*

> *For if you forgive men their trespasses, your heavenly Father will also forgive you (Matthew 6:14).*

> *A man that has friends must himself be friendly (Proverbs 18:24).*

We do not envy the wealthy man when we see that all men hate him. We may long for his wealth, but we recognize that to lose relationships with people is to be really poor. This is an oft-neglected area of wealth that is overlooked in our pursuit of goods and chattels.

People, who have gained respect, have many friends and close relationships. They have trust in others who trust in them, and they pursue a loving family and a good name. They are truly wealthy. They possess something of great value, greater than material wealth, which cannot be bought even with a great price.

Four Points To Consider

We must realize that our notions of wealth are very limited and polluted by the value system of the world. We are more likely to think of goods as indicators of wealth and to put value on things that can be sold for a price, but the greatest wealth this life offers is found in things that cannot be bought or sold with gold or silver. They are the things that must be gained by living in a right relationship with God, fully submitted to His will. What most people consider to be wealth is poverty in the light of these true riches.

Gaining true wealth and riches is a product of Christ's character and a correct life-style before God. It's hard work and it makes strong demands on us. Developing the character of Christ requires the death of our flesh nature. But the rewards are great, and they are the only real rewards anyway. There are those who have amassed supposed wealth but died alone and in misery for lack of true riches. There are those who have had none of this world's goods, but nonetheless were fabulously wealthy in the treasures that really satisfy.

Point #1: Develop meekness.
We need to develop meekness by taking charge of our lives through the Spirit's power, and entering into the kind of obedience that causes our flesh to complain. By so doing, we begin to inherit the earth, and its treasures become ours to enjoy.

Point #2: Become poor in spirit.
We must develop poverty of spirit, no longer relying on ourselves but totally submitting to God as our only Lord

and source. We must see ourselves as impoverished, needy and of no value to ourselves. By doing so, we begin to possess the Kingdom of God and its treasures become ours to enjoy.

Point #3: Become committed to righteousness.
We must become committed to righteousness to such an extent that the unrighteous persecute us for standing for what is right. By doing so, we also access the kingdom of heaven.

Point #4: Invest in others.
We ought to make a correct and biblical investment in others: showing mercy and forgiveness, and being gracious and friendly. Doing this, we receive those very things in return and enjoy the best of healthy and loving relationships.

– 3 –

The Curse of Covetousness

A great hindrance to receiving God's blessing is the reluctance to deal with covetousness. Covetousness is considered so important that it's included in the Ten Commandments. That commandment not only says, "Thou shall not covet," as in the brief, simple language of the other commandments, but it also lists the things that we are often tempted to covet:

You shall not covet your neighbor's house; you shall not covet your neighbor's wife, nor his male servant, nor his female servant, nor his ox, nor his donkey, nor anything that is your neighbor's (Exodus 20:17).

Despite this strict and detailed ban by God, covetousness has become the driving force behind our western economies and a major preoccupation in much of our lives. To keep the wheels of industry turning, western economies require that we consume. To induce consumption, a multimillion-dollar advertising and promotions industry has developed for no other purpose than to appeal to our covetousness. Elaborate and compelling television advertisements are constantly invented to draw upon the natural instinct to please ourselves. Desires are wakened, not to live godly or to give ourselves to God's service, but to possess something for ourselves and thus gratify our own desires.

Our ability to covet needs no provocation because the natural human state is one of lusting. We are addicted to the *"lust of the flesh, the lust of the eyes, and the pride of life"* (1 John 2:16). Covetousness is the disease of this age. It is built into our nature and encouraged by more powerful devices today than at any other time in history.

The Example of Achan

Through the story of Achan and the destruction of Jericho, in Joshua 7, God revealed an important truth about covetousness that we all must heed. Before going into battle against the walled city of Jericho, Israel was told by God that the contents of the city were cursed. Everything was to be destroyed except for the silver and gold and the brass and iron vessels. These were to be taken into God's treasury (Joshua 6:17-19).

One of the Israelite men, Achan, disobeyed God's commandment and took for himself gold, silver and a Babylonian garment, which he hid in his tent. No one knew of Achan's sin, except God.

Achan had successfully gotten away with his covetousness. No one saw what was in his heart, and he had the goods safely hidden away. It wasn't until Joshua and his men were defeated in their attempt to take the city of Ai that they realized something was terribly wrong. God's explanation was that, *"Israel has sinned, and they have also transgressed My covenant which I commanded them"* (Joshua 7:11). God saw Achan's sin as a blot on the whole nation. One man's disobedient actions brought suffering upon the entire nation.

Israel's defeat at Ai had nothing to do with military might or strategy, but everything to do with the sinful state of one man who had disobeyed God. God explained to Joshua that this defeat resulted from sin, making Israel accursed. God then declared, *"Neither will I be with you anymore, unless you destroy the accursed from among you"* (Joshua 7:12).

Early the next day Joshua assembled all the tribes of Israel to present themselves before him. The tribe of Judah was selected by casting lots, and then the family lines were progressively followed until Achan was selected. Once exposed, Achan confessed his sin and said, *"When I saw among the spoils a beautiful Babylonian garment, two hundred shekels of silver, and a wedge of gold weighing fifty shekels, then I **coveted** them, and took them"* (Joshua 7:21, emphasis added).

Achan confessed to covetousness. Nevertheless, Achan and his family were stoned to death and buried under a huge pile of rocks, together with his flocks, his possessions, and the items he took from Jericho. Then, and only then, were the people of Israel free from Achan's sin.

> Covetousness isn't something that God takes lightly.

This graphic statement of God's attitude toward covetousness demonstrates that it's not a private sin that we can allow into our heart to be dealt with some day in the future. Covetousness is not even a personal sin. It affects all those around us who will also come under the curse of God on account of our sin. Covetousness isn't something that God takes lightly. God's judgment on Achan is sobering indeed, and is reinforced by His judgment on a husband and wife hundreds of years later.

Ananias and Sapphira sold land and decided to keep some of the money for themselves. By itself, that wasn't a crime; they were allowed to do so if they chose. However, they decided to keep a portion for themselves while giving the impression they were giving it all to God. They were being deceptive for personal gain. Their judgment came quickly as they were struck dead at Peter's feet (Acts 5:1-10).

Covetousness is a matter of supreme importance in God's frame of reference. Most likely God's reason for not allowing the collection of personal spoil at Jericho was to challenge the hearts of His people. He wanted to expose and cleanse the covetousness that existed in the nation. It certainly did expose the covetousness of Achan, who was dealt with most severely.

The Things We Covet

The story of Achan's covetousness suggests the types of coveting to which we fall prey. First, there were the worldly goods of Babylon as represented by the Babylonian garment. Then there were the goods dedicated to God as represented by the silver and gold. You can see that Achan coveted both.

Coveting The Things of the World

We can be guilty of coveting this world's goods, which is where most people are found guilty. We want the world's finery and are attracted to its treasures. This is especially so because these things are constantly paraded before our eyes by the advertising media. We are told in a hundred compelling ways that the surest way to happiness, contentment and fulfillment is to possess these things. If we have them, we believe we are certainly blessed.

Coveting the world's goods must be dealt with in no uncertain terms. We are not permitted to have lustful, covetous longing for the things of this world. This is a trap, because we are to set our affections on things above, not on the things of this earth (Colossians 3:2). Yet how many of us are guilty of spending our lives and resources absorbed in attempting to gain another portion of this world's goods?

It is significant that Achan's covetousness caused him to take a Babylonian garment. In contrast, Scripture speaks of the garments God's people are to wear a *"garment of praise,"* *"garments of salvation"* and a *"robe of righteousness"* (Isaiah 61:3-10). To clothe ourselves with the world's goods involves stripping away the garments God has provided for us.

This is dramatically shown in Revelation 3:14-18 where the church of the Laodicea became distracted by a love for worldly goods. They said of themselves, "I am rich, have become wealthy, and have need of nothing." Wealth was the focal point of their hearts. In the face of the positive and boastful notions about their own prosperity, God declared them, "wretched, miserable, poor, blind and NAKED." They saw themselves clothed in this world's finery, but that made them spiritually naked. They were not clothed with the garments of praise, salvation or righteousness.

God instructed them to buy from Him the things of true value so that they may be CLOTHED and the shame of their nakedness covered:

> *"I counsel you to buy from Me gold refined in the fire, that you may be rich; and white garments, that you may be clothed, that the shame of your nakedness may not be revealed; and anoint your eyes with eye salve, that you may see" (Revelation 3:18).*

We cannot pursue the things of this world without stripping ourselves of the provisions of God. Jesus put it simply, *"You cannot serve God and mammon"* (Matthew 6:24).

The church at Laodicea accumulated goods by worldly methods, and put value on things with no real value. They had a false sense of that which was precious and that which was profane. They deceived themselves into thinking that the world's standards were the true measurements of value. However, value is not determined by supply and demand or the worth attributed to things by people.

There is a value system completely independent of the concepts of worth assigned by man. This value system gives things their real, lasting and eternal value. The Laodicean church failed to look to God for confirmation of what had value and what was empty vanity. They lusted after the things their hearts desired, unaware that the Spirit of God saw no value at all in their accumulated possessions.

We saw in the previous chapter that God's people are supposed to "inherit the earth." But we are not to accumulate goods by worldly methods or put value on things that God considers of no lasting value. We must set our affections on things above, not on things of the earth (Colossians 3:2).

"Do not lay up for yourselves treasures on earth, where moth and rust destroy and where thieves break in and steal, but lay up for yourselves treasures in heaven, where neither moth nor rust destroys and where thieves do not break in and steal. For where your treasure is, there your heart will be also" (Matthew 6:19-21).

Coveting What Belongs to God

We discovered from the story of Achan that we can be guilty of coveting what belongs to God. Achan did when he took the silver and gold designated for the Lord's treasury. Instead of yielding to God that which is God's we are often inclined to possess it for ourselves. We may be tempted to withhold the tithe or a gift God is asking from us. We can covet the praise that belongs to God, the property and wealth that belongs to God, or even the claim on our lives that God deserves.

Withholding from God is robbery. The only place in Scripture where God speaks about being "robbed" is in reference to withholding the tithe and offering:

> *"Will a man rob God? Yet you have robbed Me! But you say, 'In what way have we robbed You?' In tithes and offerings. You are cursed with a curse, For you have robbed Me, Even this whole nation"* *(Malachi 3:8-9).*

You could distinguish what belonged to Caesar, because Caesar's image and superscription was on it. Similarly, you can know what belongs to God because those things are made in God's image. In other words, we have an irrevocable obligation to yield our lives to God, because we are the only creatures created in God's image. When we purpose in our hearts to live for ourselves, please ourselves, go where we want to go and do what we want to do, we are taking possession of what belongs to God. When we ponder what we want for ourselves, we are coveting our own future and livelihood.

> *"Or do you not know that your body is the temple of the Holy Spirit who is in you, whom you have from God, and you are not your own? For you were bought at a price; therefore glorify God in your body and in your spirit, which are God's"* *(1 Corinthians 6:19-20).*

Possessing our own life is so much a part of our thinking that we are in awe and dread of the thought of God actually moving in and taking over our plans. When we meet people who have had the plans for their lives overturned by God and failed to achieve what society worships as success and accomplishment, we tend to feel genuine sympathy for them. We see them as the unlucky ones who have become victims of God's plans. Actually, we should rejoice, because God can then bring about His will and purposes.

Never forget that God's will and purposes for our lives are far greater than our own and always for our best interest. We are the Lord's, and when He takes possession of us and has His way in us, even if it upsets everything our human hearts desire, something precious and wonderful has taken place.

Defrauding

This brings us to another aspect of covetousness—the practice of withholding or "defrauding." This is the process of holding on to what we should have given to another in an attempt to possess it for ourselves.

It's surprising how ready we are to take possession of the things that belong to others. It may be that we are slow to return something borrowed, or we forgot who loaned it to us. It may be that we defer repayment of a loan to a time more convenient for us. We may withhold praise and acknowledgment from someone who genuinely earned it but for whom we hold no fondness. In a thousand different ways, our culture is involved in countless forms of defrauding others.

The Law says:
> *"You shall not defraud your neighbor, nor rob him. The wages of him who is hired shall not remain with you all night until the morning"* *(Leviticus 19:13).*

It's wrong to hold onto what rightly belongs to someone else, even if only for the night. Psalm 37:21 declares that, *"The wicked borrows and does not repay, but the righteous shows mercy and gives."* The next verse (v. 22) explains why this distinction exists. *"For those who are blessed by Him shall inherit the earth, but those who are cursed by Him shall be cut off."*

If you know you have God's blessing to inherit the earth, you could easily afford to be most generous. Whatever you give away would be only the smallest portion of your wealth. But if you know in your heart that you are wicked and cursed by God and the earth is withholding its fruit, you would resort to theft and defrauding in an effort to amass goods for yourself. You would fear the loss of the few things you possessed.

Paul wrote, *"that no one should take advantage of and defraud his brother in this matter"* (1 Thessalonians 4:6). The word defraud refers to a covetous interest in another man's goods.

> If you know you have God's blessing to inherit the earth, you could easily afford to be most generous.

Jesus used a different Greek word for defrauding when He summarized the Ten Commandments for the rich young ruler in Mark 10:19. This word translates as the phrase, *"Do not defraud"* and speaks of holding back by fraud. So the biblical concept of covetousness is closely linked to the action of defrauding one another.

All cheating, taking advantage of others, deceitful dealings, unfair pricing, deceitful weights and measures, and similar activities are the products of a covetous heart. The alternative is a heart filled with trust in God, fully confident that He will supply all your needs according to His riches in Christ Jesus. What He deems to be good for you is truly of the greatest value. This heart attitude finds no advantage in defrauding another. But if your heart lusts for the things belonging to others, you will take advantage of opportunities to add their possessions to your own.

The Example of Onan

A biblical account of defrauding is conveyed in Genesis 38:6-10. Judah's firstborn son, Er, was given a wife named Tamar. Because Er was wicked in the sight of the Lord, God killed him. Judah then asked his second son Onan to marry Tamar so that she could bear children to claim Er's inheritance. Onan began to comply, but when it came to the point of giving Tamar a child, Onan spilled his seed on the ground. By this action, he defrauded Tamar of a child, and his older brother of seed and the lawful inheritance. God was so displeased with this act of defrauding that He killed Onan.

Most likely there was little love lost between the two brothers. Er was wicked in the sight of God. Therefore, he had probably created a lot of trouble and strife, or in some way antagonized his brother, Onan.

We may be inclined to feel sympathetic toward Onan's case. Surely, it was only natural for Er to resent having to raise up children for his brother. But he was instructed to do so by his father, and God considered his refusal worthy of the death penalty.

Defrauding in Marriage

Paul instructed married people not to defraud one another sexually.

> *"Defraud ye not one the other, except it be with consent for a time, that ye may give yourselves to fasting and prayer; and come together again, that Satan tempt you not for your incontinency"* (1 Corinthians 7:5 KJV).

Paul instructed husbands and wives to recognize that the married partner has full rights to the body of their spouse.

The wife does not have authority over her own body, but the husband does. Likewise the husband does not have authority over his own body, but the wife does.

Withholding your body from your spouse defrauds them. Husbands defraud their wives when they withhold love:
> *"Husbands, love your wives, just as Christ also loved the church, and gave Himself for it" (Ephesians 5:25).*

Husbands also defraud their wives when they withhold the due consideration they are instructed to give:
> *"Likewise you husbands, dwell with them with understanding, giving honor to the wife, as to the weaker vessel, and as being heirs together of the grace of life, that your prayers may not be hindered" (1 Peter 3:7).*

Wives defraud their husbands when they withhold the submission (respectful response) they are instructed to give:
> *"Wives, submit to your own husbands, as to the Lord" (Ephesians 5:22).*

When we become preoccupied with our own concerns in life at the expense of time with our families, we are defrauding them of what is rightfully theirs. If we withhold godly discipline from our children, we are defrauding them from developing the godly character intended by God. In many different ways we defraud others of what is rightly theirs.

A Warning to Defrauders

When we defraud someone, through our selfishness or thoughtlessness, we put ourselves in a dangerous position. God avenges on behalf of those who have been the victims of fraud.

> *"That no one should take advantage and defraud his*
> *brother in this matter, because the Lord is the avenger*
> *of all such, as we also forewarned you and testified"*
> *(1 Thessalonians 4:6).*

If you are the defrauder, then God will have to deal with you.

The Jericho Covetousness Test

We do not qualify for the blessings of God so long as there is any covetousness in our hearts. That is the point of the Jericho restriction.

God told the Israelites they were not to take spoils from the city, except to collect what God claimed for Himself. After forty years of limited resources and an absence of worldly wealth, they found themselves confronted with an abundance of luxurious and tempting goodies. God told them they couldn't have any of it. The plunder was either to be put aside for God or destroyed. This was God's "covetousness test" for the children of Israel. He wanted them to have pure hearts toward Him and not be distracted by the world's goods.

Sharing the Curse

Only one man, Achan, failed this test. He was drawn aside by his own lusts and tempted. Achan's covetousness was aroused, and he didn't fear God enough to be wise about the way he responded. He disobeyed God and thereby unintentionally brought a curse on the entire nation.

Achan believed that his actions were his own secret, personal business. He had no objection to the other people following and obeying God's instructions. Nevertheless, his secret actions of self-interest brought destruction upon everyone else.

So it is today. Our actions of covetousness and self-interest are not simply between God and ourselves. The popular belief today is that if people agree among themselves to do certain acts and others will not be hurt, then those acts aren't considered wrong. People assume that if their actions don't hurt anyone, they are their own private business and don't affect the lives of others.

However, God sees sin as a blot against the entire people among whom the sin exists. When people down the street from you become involved in godless activities, they bring God's judgment upon your community and your nation. You cannot assume a "head in the sand" attitude. It's not valid and never has been. *"Righteousness exalts a nation, but sin is a reproach to any people"* (Proverbs 14:34).

Achan was the only man to take forbidden goods, and what he took from Jericho was only a fraction of its wealth. Nevertheless, his actions resulted in the death of fellow Israelites when the nation went into its next battle.

The Contrast with Ai

God had declared that the contents of Jericho were cursed, and said, *"Keep yourselves from accursed things, lest you become accursed"* (Joshua 6:18). Yet in Ai, the next city taken by Israel, they were allowed to collect as much of the spoils as they chose. God had one standard for Jericho and another for Ai. God withholds sanctioned blessings until we have dealt with the covetousness in our hearts. Jericho was Israel's "covetousness test." The only one who coveted and had not feared the Lord was destroyed, thereby cleansing the nation of this sin. Thereafter, Israel was free to take the spoils from the next cities. The abundance was theirs.

God regards covetousness as a very serious matter. It was not a minor suggestion when God said, *"You shall not covet."* He wants the heart attitude toward wealth and possessions dealt with and purified. Only after covetousness has been put to death will God allow you to possess freely the things He has prepared.

Distinguishing Between Various Forms of Wealth

Covetousness causes one to indiscriminately desire the world's goods. God made distinctions, and declared some of the world's goods accursed, but declared others to be inoffensive to Him. If we are walking in covetousness, we will not make that distinction. All wealth will seem equal, no matter how it is attained. Those who walk with God will hear His voice on the matter and know what He is blessing and what He is cursing. In the fear of God, they will keep themselves from those things they desire but not blessed by God.

However, many Christians today are financial opportunists, chasing one scheme and opportunity after another. They pray about their deals and ask for God's blessing, but their various pursuits only devour their time and resources without yielding the expected return. This is the fruit of chasing after the lusts of the heart and latching onto whatever promises to provide the desired end. God may be asking us to work at something that produces a far smaller return, but one covered by His blessing. If these Christians were truly seeking God's will and weren't motivated by covetousness, they would find greater fruitfulness from less exciting opportunities sent and blessed of God. How easily we deceive and injure ourselves.

Covetous Preachers

Sadly, some preachers are ready to manipulate and take advantage of the covetousness in the hearts of God's people.

Covetous preachers who want to build a following preach things that tickle the ears of their covetous hearers. They entice people to make unwise investments in ministries and hasty contributions not endorsed by God.

This causes people to become bad stewards of God's blessings. They think that because their covetous investment goes into a ministry instead of a business, God must bless it. In this case, God's people (the hearers) are oppressed by those (the preachers) who worship gain more earnestly than they do.

Covetous Adultery

The issue of covetousness is addressed in James 4:2-4. James informs us that we fail to possess because of lust. He says that we fight and struggle to gain, but fail because we only want those things that appease our lusts. Even when we come to God and ask for His provision, we don't receive it because our motivation is lustful. This is called adultery, because our hearts have gone after this world instead of after God.

> Until we deal with covetousness, we labor under the curse placed upon this world's goods.

Covetousness must be dealt with before we will see God's blessings on our life. We must face the test of Jericho and deal with covetousness in order to collect the blessings at Ai.

Until we deal with covetousness, we labor under the curse placed upon this world's goods. When we covet something, it becomes a cursed thing. We may be coveting that which belongs to man or to God—it makes no difference. The things we possess will curse us until we repent of covetousness and turn away from it.

Possessiveness

We have demonstrated that covetousness is revealed by the act of defrauding others. It is also identified by the way in which we possess the things that do not rightfully belong to us. Consider this example:
A woman once came to me seeking prayer for arthritis.

I asked her: "What are you anxious about?"

She blurted out, "My husband pays too much attention to other people's children and not our own. He's always doing something for other people's children, and he's neglecting our own children."

I responded with a challenge.

"Who told you they were YOUR children? Those children are God's heritage. They belong to the Lord. You certainly have a responsibility to the children, but they are not your children. You are getting worried about something that you have no right to get worried about because you haven't committed them back to the One who really owns them."

Possessiveness is a significant aspect of covetousness. Once something has come into our possession, we have a strong tendency to hold on to it tightly. That's why people suspect the church is trying to get THEIR money. We see our spouse, children, home and family as OURS, instead of God's property entrusted into our care.

Three Steps to Conquer Covetousness

I trust you now understand why covetousness has absolutely no place in the life of a Christian. Not only are you to behave more reasonably than sinners, but you are to be transformed in your life-style as well. This is demonstrated by doing the works of the Father, and despising and putting to death the works of your flesh. Covetousness is sin, no matter what form it takes—outright lust and greed, defrauding or possessiveness—and it must go.

Step 1: Repentance

God asks that we come to Him and repent for allowing covetousness to have a place in our lives. We need to recognize it for what it is: ugly, destructive, and unrighteous, and a curse, and pollution to your Christian life. Rid your heart of it. Put right anything and everything that you have defrauded from another. Determine in your heart to never again touch the accursed thing, and never again covet what belongs to this world, to another person or to God Himself.

Step 2: Restoration

Restore a godly attitude toward the things in your possession. **Hold on to them lightly.** Focus your attention on the things given to you in trust. Do not be possessive, but a good steward. You don't own your job, your family, money, talents, home, ministry, opportunities or anything else that God has placed into your hands. Care for them on His behalf. Attend to these as one committed to serving God, and always be ready and willing to yield them back to God at any moment without complaint.

Step 3: Restitution

Clean out the attic. Allow the Spirit of God to remind you of things you've collected over the years that don't belong to you. Make restitution when impressed to do so by the Lord. Put right everything you have allowed to remain unsettled. Empty your hands of everything collected that is not rightfully yours. God will then fill your hands with the blessed things, which are His reward.

Finally, remember that the Lord will bless you as you earnestly seek His will.

Stewardship

Properly understanding wealth and possessions involves insight and revelation of the principle of stewardship. It is not a concept easily embraced, because it denies us the right of ownership. People are naturally covetous at heart. The truth is simply this: No matter how unpleasant an instruction may be, when it's God's plan and purpose, it leads to great blessing.

Stewardship is the true purpose of man's role on the earth. Unless you become a steward at heart, you will never know the wonder of God's blessings. Stewardship is the opposite spirit of covetousness. Just as covetousness brings a curse, stewardship brings a blessing upon everything we hold in trust.

The psalmist wrote a foundational text for stewardship:
"The earth is the LORD's, and all its fullness, the world, and those who dwell therein" (Psalm 24:1).

This verse informs us who owns everything. God does. Therefore, if God owns everything, how much of it is yours? None! The only way to get any of it is through inheritance from God. Otherwise, you only have the use of it as a loan from the owner, God.

When we are given the use of something that doesn't belong to us, we serve as a steward of that thing. We are completely responsible to the owner for how we treat it, and are accountable for how we use it.

Man's Gift of Sustenance

Looking back to the beginning of creation, we discover that although God made the earth for mankind to dwell in, He did not give the earth to man. Man was given use of the earth and given instructions about how to treat it honorably in response to the Owner's command. Man was never given ownership of God's creation.

God's instruction to mankind is found in Genesis 1:28-29: *"Be fruitful and multiply, fill the earth and subdue it, and take authority over the animals."* We also learn in this passage that the only thing God gave man from the creation to possess and use for himself was food from the plant kingdom: *"I have given you every herb that yields seed which is on the face of all the earth, and every tree whose fruit yields seed; to you it shall be for food."*

The only thing that man was given was something to eat. There is nothing very lasting about food or its nutritional value. It is a vital, yet temporary substance. God demonstrated in this that temporary sustenance is all that mankind will ever get out of the earth, and it's only meant to provide what is necessary to maintain life. When we die, we take nothing out of this world: *"For we brought nothing into this world, and it is certain we can carry nothing out"* (1 Timothy 6:7).

All that we will have gained from the world is a number of days, which we also use and "consume." So in a very real sense, man is a "consumer." The most man will ever possess of the earth is the temporary sustenance that keeps him alive until it is his time to leave planet earth and meet his Maker.

But God's simple provision of food to sustain man during his period of stewardship is perverted by lust:

You lust and do not have. You murder and covet and cannot obtain. You fight and war. Yet you do not have because you do not ask. You ask and do not receive, because you ask amiss, that you may spend it on your pleasures (James 4:2-3).

Distorted Consumerism

Worldly consumerism is an exploitative and indulgent process that is not stewardship at all, but an abuse of what we are expected to hold in trust. Being a consumer, in God's plan, is not intended to be lustful self-gratification. It is meant to be the necessary meeting of the life-sustaining requirement for food. More specifically, all we are given of the earth is our daily bread. When we lay claim to more, we attempt to take from God what belongs to Him. This is why in the Lord's Prayer the only possession we are taught to request is our "daily bread" (Matthew 6:11).

> ... God designed man to be fulfilled with spiritual things.

Instead of accepting God's provision and fulfilling His calling for our lives, we've developed a craze to possess. Having lost a relationship with God, mankind tries to fill the void in life with material things. However, God designed man to be fulfilled with spiritual things.

Jesus displayed the potency of spiritual sustenance when he ministered to the woman at the well. When His disciples returned with food, Jesus declined to eat, saying that He had been nourished with food they knew not of, that is, in doing the will of the Father (John 4:31-34).

The sum total of all that this world has to offer us is nourishment. But even that is a poor substitute for the more important spiritual nourishment available through obeying the will of the Father.

So it is that when humanity lost touch with the Living God, people turned to self-gratification through consuming the world's resources. Consumption will always be a meaningless replacement for the nourishment of doing the will of God.

Stewardship and Accountability

Stewards are accountable for their stewardship. When we are given something to hold in trust, we are expected to care for it according to the owner's instruction and to yield the fruit of it to the owner.

Jesus taught this principle in the Parable of the Vineyard recorded in Matthew 21:32-41. Jesus related that the keepers of the vineyard were wicked, so when the owner sent his servants to collect the fruit of the vineyard, the keepers stoned them. When Jesus asked what the owner would do in such a situation, those listening replied:

> *"He will destroy those wicked men miserably, and lease his vineyard unto other vinedressers who will render to him the fruits in their season" (Matthew 21:41).*

Thus, stewardship is a matter to be taken seriously. Stewards are accountable and answerable to the owner. If they fail to be good stewards, they should anticipate a strict penalty. What was given them to hold in trust will be taken away and placed in the hands of another.

Notice the severity in which these stewards were judged—they were to be destroyed. This was not the sentence of a just God dealing with them out of righteous indignation. It was the assessment of the men during that time. Stewardship was taken very seriously, not only by God, but by the common people as well. No one had any doubt about the dangers involved in failing to be a good steward.

What was the servants' failure? They withheld the fruit of the vineyard from the owner. They failed to give the owner what rightfully belonged to him. Additionally, they compounded their wickedness by attacking and killing the owner's agents sent to collect the fruit. Therefore, the wicked stewards were replaced with vinedressers who would properly render the fruits to the owner. The issue was in yielding the fruit of the vineyard. The increase of the vineyard belonged to the owner and not to the stewards.

We are only stewards of the earth. Everything we have is to be held in trust for the one who placed it in our hands. The fruit of our lives belongs to the One who owns our lives, and if we misuse what belongs to Him, we should anticipate punishment and destruction. God is expecting the fruit of our lives to be surrendered to Him.

The Parable of the Talents

The principle of accountability in stewardship is amplified further in Jesus' Parable of the Talents in Matthew 25:14-30. In this parable, a man delivered various amounts of money (talents) to his servants for them to be stewards over while he went on a long journey. The talents were distributed according to the varying abilities of the servants. One received five talents, one received two talents, and another received one talent.

It must be mentioned here before going any further that the master was kind and benevolent. The servants had nothing, deserved nothing and had no claim on their master. Yet, in his kindness, he gave them money out of his own pocket for their comfort, advantage and salvation. The master was also wise in that he distributed the talents according to the ability of each servant. The master made no demand on the servants for a particular amount of return on the talents entrusted to them.

During the master's absence, the first two servants put their master's money to work and doubled the original sum given to them. The servant who received only one talent, however, decided to bury it in the ground for safekeeping. When the master returned from his journey, the two who had doubled their money joyfully presented their productivity to the master and were praised for their efforts. When the third servant returned the original talent with no increase, the master became angry and punished that servant, calling him wicked, slothful and unprofitable.

Notice the sin of the unprofitable servant. He was ungrateful and ignored the mercy of the master. Instead of working to improve what he had received, he was idle. Notice his error in hiding the talent, rendering the mercy of the master to no effect. Notice his injustice in taking his master's money and doing nothing with it all the while living on the generosity intended for faithful servants. This servant's reasoning and accusation was that the master was a "hard man," which was absurd and a wicked excuse for his faithlessness. The servant was condemned by his own mouth and had refused the happiness the master had offered to him.

As punishment for the great sin of this servant, the talent entrusted to him was taken away and given to the servant who now had ten talents. He was reproached by the master and called a "wicked and slothful servant." Then the unprofitable servant was cast into outer darkness where there was weeping and gnashing of teeth. He was to have nothing but darkness and misery because he had refused to walk in the light.

Several principles must be considered from this parable:

1. Failing to be a profitable steward brings severe punishment.

2. The servants did not own the talents, but could use them as long as they remained good stewards.

3. Any profit they made belonged to the master.

4. Their reward was the master's approval, promises, blessings and the invitation to enter into the joy of the Lord.

> ... if we don't make good use of what God gives us, we don't get to keep it.

This is not just an object lesson from Jesus. This is a description of the Kingdom of Heaven. Jesus said, *"The kingdom of heaven is likened unto...."* Therefore, the purpose of the parable is to teach us God's methods of doing business in His Kingdom.

A popular principle taught through this parable is summed up in the expression, "use it or lose it." This points out that if we don't make good use of what God gives us, we don't get to keep it. This includes insights and knowledge, abilities, gifts, and skills given to us by God, all of which are to be used for His Kingdom.

The most important lesson of this parable is this: Whatever we have in our possession is not ours in the first place, and no matter how much we use or profit from it, we will never be the owners. We will always be in the position of stewards.

The Tests for Stewardship

God's stewards give to God what belongs to Him. Good stewards declare, "I don't own anything any more. Everything I have belongs to God!"

The first test of our stewardship is determined by the degree to which we take ownership of our possessions. Do we consider them as OURS, or do we regard them as GOD'S? What about the things in your possession? How do you speak about them? Have you committed them to the One who really owns them?

You can claim a commitment of everything to God and a total yielding of ownership, but you must still pass the "worry" test:
- Do you worry about the things in your possession?
- Do you lay awake at night thinking about what might happen to them?
- Do you fear loss, damage or theft of the things in your care?
- Are you able to release and entrust these things into the hands of the Lord, who owns them anyway?

We worry about possessions we think belong to us. We fear losing them, so we cling to them ever so tightly and become preoccupied with what our hearts treasure.

What about you? When your mind is at rest, to what does it turn? What affection is your heart focused upon?

If you are a good steward, your heart will be focused on God. Even your casual thoughts will turn to Him and how to please Him. But if you long to possess things for yourself, your heart will turn to thoughts of possession, gain, personal betterment, fears, worries, struggles and selfishness. This is the difference between freedom and bondage.

All you are supposed to get out of this life, in terms of natural things, is your daily bread. That's why Jesus said to ask for nothing more and to have no thought for the other things (Matthew 6:25-34). When you are focused more on this world than on your daily sustenance, you've made the created thing an idol in your heart.

Isn't this the current state of western society in its pursuit of all manner of earthly things? People are preoccupied with money, family, personal goals and ambition, job, education, pleasures and a host of other things. People are exalting created things above the Creator.

> Meekness is the state wherein our life is under control.

Furthermore, in regard to food, Scripture does not endorse the indulgent and lustful attitude toward food that is a way of life in affluent societies. The fact that we are given food and food alone as our portion from the earth does not mean we should allow eating to become a major focus in our lives. Indulging our stomachs and tantalizing our taste buds are national pastimes in America and other developed nations. But nowhere in Scripture is this preoccupation supported. Focusing on food is an aspect of the lust of the flesh:
> "...those who are Christ's have crucified the flesh with its passions and desires" (Galatians 5:24).

We discussed in chapter two Jesus' promise that the meek will inherit the earth. Meekness is the state wherein our life is under control. When in control, we will not be inclined to anger, anxiety or lust. But if we feel possessive about anything, we will become angry with anyone who threatens it, and we will be anxious about protecting it. We cannot be covetous and possessive of this world's goods and meek at the same time. Furthermore, we cannot inherit the earth until we are meek and become good and faithful stewards.

> Faithfulness is what makes one a good steward.

Therefore, we must put an end to the notion that the things given into our trust belong to us. They do not. Yet, even in ministry, people speak of "my" church, "my" ministry, "my" calling, "my" gifts, etc. Being used for spiritual purposes does not sanctify things. They are sanctified by our heart attitude toward them and in yielding them back to God for His glory.

You cannot justify covetousness by a desire to become great for God or wanting money to be used for Him. You must deal with the covetousness, be a steward, and in meekness of heart go about your Father's business.

Stewardship and Faithfulness

Stewardship demands faithfulness. The key concern in stewardship, after resolving the concept of ownership (or lack of it), is faithfulness: "… *it is required in stewards that one be found faithful*" (1 Corinthians 4:2). Faithfulness is what makes one a good steward.

If you aren't faithful, then it's impossible to be a good steward. Perhaps you would be a thief or a waster, but certainly not a steward. You cannot claim to be a good steward unless you have a faithful heart. That's why the character of Christ is so important in addressing the issue of wealth and possessions. Self-interest makes you unfaithful. As long as you are seeking the interests of your flesh, you cannot be a faithful steward.

Chris was an acquaintance of mine. Many years ago, when he was employed as a sales representative, he had to choose which clients to approach on behalf of his employer. From time to time, in order to design a product to meet a customer's needs, samples would be given to Chris by the customer, which he could usually keep. Without realizing it at the time, Chris' decisions on which client to call were based more and more on his interest in the samples he may be able to collect from them. The end result was that Chris was not being a good steward of the boss's money. He wasn't out seeking the best interest of his employer, but his own interest in the collecting of samples.

Years later God challenged Chris about his self--seeking attitudes and unfaithful heart. He had to do some soul-searching and repenting, breaking the unprofitable, covetous attitudes to which he had succumbed. Actually, it was the "something for nothing" enticement that had gripped his heart. In order to seek that personal reward, everything else had taken second place. It was an important lesson in faithfulness and stewardship.

Scripture has a word for stewards who are unfaithful. They are called "unjust" in Luke 16:10. The word means wicked and unrighteous. So faithfulness is not just the highest level in a range of possibilities; you are either faithful or you are wicked in God's sight.

Progressive Stewardship

Stewardship is a process. We have already seen this in the Parable of the Talents in Matthew 25. One servant went from nothing to having five talents entrusted to him by the master. He was able to develop those five into ten. But then, because he had proven himself faithful, he was also trusted with the talent taken from the unprofitable servant. We can reasonably assume that once this servant had turned the eleven talents into twenty, he would be given the stewardship of all twenty.

Jesus taught progressive stewardship in Luke 16:10-12, giving us three principles of progress:

He who is faithful in what is least is faithful also in much: and he who is unjust in what is least is unjust also in much. Therefore if you have not been faithful in the unrighteous mammon, who will commit to your trust the true riches? And if you have not been faithful in that which is another man's who will give you what is your own?

Principle #1: Be Faithful in Small Things
Jesus taught that we must be faithful in the small things to qualify for stewardship over the greater things. The reason for this is that faithfulness is an attitude of the heart. Once we have proven our faithfulness of heart, we can be trusted with greater treasure and responsibility. But if our heart is unfaithful, we prove to be untrustworthy even in the small things.

When God gives you things-in-trust, they are essentially a test of your heart. Will you be diligent, faithful, consistent and correct in your attitude toward them?

This test often catches us unprepared. We can sometimes have the sincere belief that once we are given a challenge or responsibility of greater merit, we will rise to the occasion. This is a deception. If we cannot be faithful with the mundane, unexciting challenges, or if we do not yield ownership back to God, then our heart is proven unfaithful and unqualified for anything better.

When one has a perverse heart, it doesn't matter whether they are asked to take care of twenty cents, two hundred dollars, a message, or a simple duty, they will look for personal advantage in the situation, and will see it as "looking out for number one." However, God sees it as wickedness.

Be sure your heart is pure, and watch how you respond to the small challenges of stewardship that God sends your way.

Principle #2: Worldly Riches are a Test

The world's riches are a test to determine if we deserve the true riches. If we've been unfaithful in our handling of money, possessions, responsibilities, opportunities, and the natural issues of our life, then we do not qualify for spiritual responsibility and opportunity.

Paul confirmed this by pointing out that a man was not worthy to be an elder unless he first proved himself faithful in the natural issues presented in family life. He had to be the husband of one wife and have his family in subjection to his authority. Paul would have a hard job finding men to meet these criteria today. Society gives us permission to be unfaithful, but God's standards have not changed.

Your current life circumstances are a test for you. You can either handle them faithfully, possessing nothing and meeting God's requirements in every situation, or you can be unfaithful, self-seeking and possessive. If you prove yourself unfaithful with the issues in your life as they are now, then you had better give up all aspirations of having any true riches at your disposal.

Principle #3: Another Man's Possessions

You must prove your faithfulness with that which belongs to another before you qualify for anything of our own. The late Ed Cole, founder of the Christian Men's Network, expounded this principle by teaching that you cannot be given your own ministry until you have first been prepared by faithfully supporting and serving in someone else's ministry.

At a more fundamental level, this truth can be linked to Psalm 24:1, which says the earth is the Lord's. You must realize that every daily circumstance encountered in this world gives you an opportunity to be faithful with that which belongs to another.

> **God asked Chris, "What would you do if that is My will and calling for your life?"**

It's useless to become impatient to start your own business or ministry, or leave home to start your own family unless or until you have first proven yourself faithful to another man's business or ministry and submitted to another man's authority. Your home, your home church, and your first job are the key areas of stewardship. They are not meant to oppress you or hold you back until you have the opportunity to break out and go on your own. To the contrary, they are the times and places meant to reveal the motivations of your heart. They will either qualify you for something of your own or prove your unfaithfulness.

Chris recalled a time when, as a younger man, he was in a church serving a pastor who gave him little opportunity (in Chris' opinion) to express and develop his ministry potential. One day someone proposed that Chris would have a lifelong calling to serve under that pastor's ministry. The very suggestion brought despair to Chris's heart, but God spoke a challenging word. God asked Chris, "What would you do if that is My will and calling for your life?" Chris realized there was no alternative but to be faithful in that calling, regardless of whether or not he found it desirable. Once that matter was settled in Chris's heart, God began to prepare the way for him to move forward in ministry and eventually into a fruitful ministry of his own.

The Steward's Reward

If the good steward does not possess those things entrusted into his hands, then what does he receive for all of his effort? Is there any real reward for being a good steward?

Good stewards enjoy two rewards, and both are worth earnest pursuit: 1) the honor bestowed by the Master, and 2) the reward of position or standing.

The good stewards spoken about in Scripture were all rewarded with the praise of their master. Acknowledgment by the master also involved an endorsement for a promotion in stewardship. As these stewards proved themselves faithful in the portion measured out to them, they were allowed to progress into a higher level of stewardship and responsibility.

The second level of reward comes along with that promotion. Just as in a king's court, there were those who dined with the king at his table, those who ate at the servants' table, and others who ate at the doorstep. The portions measured to those stewards depended upon their level of promotion. If a once trusted steward proved to be unfaithful, he might find himself stripped of rank and reduced to the meager rations of a stable hand. Another steward, by proving himself faithful, could move up in responsibility and enjoy all the privileges and new delights of his improved station in life.

Scripture indicates that these rewards are part of God's Kingdom plan as well. Consider these examples:

> *His lord said unto him, well done, good and faithful servant; you were faithful over a few things, I will make you ruler over many things.* ***Enter into the joy of your lord*** *(Matthew 25:21, 23 emphasis added).*

Blessed are those servants whom the master, when he comes, will find watching. Assuredly, I say unto you that he (the LORD) will gird himself and have them to sit down to eat, and will come and serve them (Luke 12:37).

And the Lord said, who then is that faithful and wise steward, whom his master will make ruler over his household, to give them their portion of food in due season? (Luke 12:42).

Proving to be faithful as a steward brings great reward. The Master will feed you Himself. The portion that's yours to consume will become all the more joyous as it comes closer and closer to the portion the Master Himself enjoys. Don't try to find joy and satisfaction through indulgence. Set yourself upon pleasing the Lord in faithfulness and with the heart of a true steward. Then you will have joy unspeakable and be full of glory.

Are You Ready for Stewardship?

Stewardship is serious business. It is not something that must be endured by unfortunate ones who don't have what it takes to be their own lord and master. Rather, stewardship is essential for all of us, for all of our lives. From our birth until our dying breath, we are stewards over the world's provisions. And that stewardship is our greatest opportunity. If we set our heart right and take on the heart of a steward, we can advance into the very best this world offers, not with possessiveness, but to hold in trust for God.

– 5 –

God's People and Caring

G od expects His people to be givers through three basic expressions. These expressions of giving are separate and not to be confused with each other, and they teach us three important attitudes toward money.

Expression #1: Offerings made unto God.
We recognize that everything we have belongs to God, so we should have a heart to give to God whatever and whenever we can. This giving is an expression of worship and is a statement of affection and our focus on Him. It also recognizes that because all of our possessions belong to God anyway, we shouldn't hold onto them too tightly.

Expression #2: The tithe.
This is a specific kind of giving based on the revelation that one-tenth of everything God entrusts to us belongs specifically to Him. It is to be given back, through our hands, into the Lord's work for the advancement of His Kingdom on earth. The people gave the tithe to God's servants for the work of the religious leaders. This giving had a threefold effect by:

    1. challenging the giver to acknowledge God's ownership of their material possessions

2. keeping the servants of God accountable to the people

3. making the leaders reliant on the heart condition of God's people

Expression #3: Giving to the poor.

Jesus said that we would always have the poor with us (Matthew 26:11). The problem of poverty will never be solved, so we will never be released from the godly obligation to give freely and generously to those worse off than ourselves. Scripture is clear about what we need to do:

• The Jews were to leave their land untended every seventh year for the benefit of the poor and needy (Exodus 23:11).

• The rich young ruler, who claimed obedience to all the laws of God, was told to go and sell all that he had and give it to the poor (Matthew 19:21).

• We are warned not to harden our hearts or close our hands toward the poor (Deuteronomy 15:7).

• When we give to the poor, we are lending to the Lord (Proverbs 19:17).

• Paul declared that he was committed to giving to the poor (Galatians 2:10).

Jesus was totally committed to giving to the poor. This was such a normal function of the ministry that when Judas, as ministry treasurer, went out to betray Jesus, some of the disciples assumed he was going out to give money to the poor (John 13:26-29). Obviously, for such an assumption to be made, Jesus must have often sent Judas to take money to the needy.

Catching a quick overview of these three areas of giving, we note the heart of the matter—a realization that our possessions do not belong to us but are entrusted to us for the benefit of God and others, as well as for ourselves. This is the essence of stewardship:

1. We are to give of the money and possessions in our power as an expression of our worship and devotion to God, facilitating the advancement of God's kingdom here on earth. The building of the tabernacle and the temple, upkeep of the system of worship, repair of the temple, and upkeep of prophets and men of God were all made possible by generous freewill offerings.

2. The tithe was given to feed and provide for the ministers of God. God's ordered system of worship and spiritual ministry was maintained by the regular tithes of the people. The priests were also able to benefit from the offerings brought to God, to supplement the tithes they received, but the tithe was an essential part of God's plan.

3. Giving to the poor reminds us that we are all created beings and that God loves and cares for the less fortunate as much as for those with more material blessings. In a completely unselfish and non-covetous way, we are to share the blessings we have received from God with those who are in need. We may have little to share and there may be wealthier people with more ability to contribute, but we are still under divine obligation to give.

The Specific Instruction to Give

A fourth category of giving is giving in obedience. The tithe already belongs to God, and if we do not give it, we are robbing God, but the other two areas are matters of our free will. We can choose whether to give an offering to God, and we can choose whether to give to the poor. There are promises and blessing attached to all of the first three of areas of giving.

The fourth area, giving in obedience, is not one of free will. It is obeying a specific instruction from God. The widow at Zarephath was commanded by God to feed Elijah. Her subsequent actions suggest that she was hoping to eat the last of her food before the prophet arrived, but she obeyed God's command and was miraculously provided for until the end of the drought (1 Kings 17:16). This was not an offering, a tithe, or freewill giving to the poor. It was a commandment, directed specifically to a person chosen by God. It was an enormous challenge of faith but also contained a great blessing in the obedience.

> **From time to time we will be prompted by the Holy Spirit to give.**

From time to time we will be prompted by the Holy Spirit to give. This prompting may come as direct instructions, which we are to obey. The prompting may seem to come at an inopportune time, and may require great faith in addition to the obedience. However, the example of the widow at Zarephath encourages us to expect a special provision from God when His directions are heeded. Peter was asked to make a provision for Jesus by lending his boat to the Master so He could use it to preach from. Peter's obedience was rewarded by Jesus with a record catch of fish.

Giving is Natural and Blessed

Giving shouldn't be a "big deal" for the people of God, but simply an extension of their total commitment. Giving should be done freely and with no internal or personal upheaval, because Christians are meek and have crucified the flesh with its passions and lusts. Covetousness should have no rule over them, because their hearts are not set on the things of earth but on the things of heaven.

Christians should see themselves as stewards of God's wonderful provisions. They know their possessions belong to God, so they'll have no problem returning them to Him or passing them on to others as prompted to do so. The giving hearts of Christians activate the miraculous provisions of God.

When God's people know how to give, they release God's intended stream of blessing:

Give, and it will be given you: good measure, pressed down, shaken together, and running over will be put into your bosom. For with the same measure that you use, it will be measured back to you (Luke 6:38).

Honor the Lord with your possessions, and with the first-fruit of all your increase; So your barns will be filled with plenty, and your vats will overflow with new wine (Proverbs 3:9-10).

With a right heart toward God, and therefore a right heart toward possessions and stewardship, God's people fulfill His laws of prosperity. They don't give in order to gain a return, because as soon as they use God's laws for personal gain, they've given into covetousness and their hearts are corrupted.

God's prosperity pattern is based on giving and planting: Give, and it will be given to you... (Luke 6:38).

He who sows sparingly will also reap sparingly, and he who sows bountifully will also reap bountifully (2 Corinthians 9:6).

The apostle Paul underscored the fact that giving should be the life-style of Christians by linking our giving with the agricultural principle of planting seed to grow a crop. Our gifts to God's work are the seeds, which provide us with a time of reaping.

The link between our actions and the blessed result is probably nowhere emphasized more strongly than in our giving to God and His abundant giving back to us. The verses used above indicate this response on God's part:

> *"It will be given to you," "It will be measured to you again," "...will not lack," "your barns be filled with plenty," "reap bountifully."*

As the old expression says, "You cannot outgive God."

We also have a promise of reward in the tithe, though we are only returning to God what is His:

> *"'Bring all the tithes into the storehouse, That there may be food in My house, And try Me now in this,' Says the LORD of hosts, 'If I will not open for you the windows of heaven And pour out for you such blessing That there will not be room enough to receive it'"* (Malachi 3:10).

Today, these Scriptures are often connected with the prospect of giving in order to get. Much of what is called the "Prosperity Doctrine" appeals to covetousness in both the hearts of the preachers who promise surefire results by contributing to their ministries, and in the hearts of the people who give, expecting to receive personal gain. Paul, however, warned against being motivated by covetousness.

Before Paul gives the principle of sowing and reaping in 2 Corinthians 9:6 (KJV), he explains that he wants the people to give *"as a matter of bounty, and not out of covetousness."* The word "bounty" in this passage means "blessing." In other words, give to bless and not to get blessed.

The underlying attitude that we must have concerning the question of giving is to perceive our wealth as something being held in trust. Otherwise, it's of no value to anything except our covetousness. Once we have cleansed our hearts of covetousness, we can release the money or other possessions entrusted to us for the purposes that please God.

A Closer Look at the Future

Before closing this chapter, we must examine more closely the question of the tithe. Some churches teach that the tithe is a principle of God, while others suggest that it is an Old Testament law not binding to the New Testament church.

The tithe first appears in Scripture as a spontaneous act of worship on the part of Abraham, who tithed the spoils of war to Melchizedek (Genesis 14:18-20). There was no legal requirement here, but only the actions of a man whose heart was committed in worship to God.

Prior to this, there were spontaneous offerings made to God as similar acts of worship. The fact that these freewill sacrifices and offerings were incorporated into Jewish law does nothing to negate their long-term importance or relevance. If they had been was destroyed, or indeed had never been established in the first place, we would still have in Scripture the phenomenon of the tithe as the response of a loving heart toward God.

The tithe is the only thing referred to in Scripture that was robbed from God by His people (Malachi 3:8). God's people brought blemished offerings because they had adulterous hearts, but the notion of theft was never applied to those actions. While bringing an improper offering was polluting God's altar, withholding the tithe was robbery. God holds His ownership of the tithe in high regard.

God declared in Leviticus 27:30:
> *"All the tithe of the land, whether of the seed of the land or of the fruit of the tree, is the LORD's: it is holy to the LORD."*

God also claimed the tithe of their flocks and herds, declaring that one-tenth was His. Once something belonged to Him, it was not to be swapped or tampered with, for it was holy unto the Lord (Leviticus 27:32-33).

The implication of Scripture is that everyone must tithe, no matter how little they have. Some preachers think they must avoid teaching on giving and tithing to people who are very poor. However, God's Word makes no distinction between the rich and the poor regarding tithing. We must all yield a tithe to the Lord, because it is His and He requires it.

Many are teaching today that to tithe is to bring ourselves back under the law, and therefore under the curse of the law. As we study the New Testament, we see that as a part of His Kingdom teaching, Jesus endorsed tithing, not condemned it.
> *"For ye pay tithe on mint and anise and cumin, and have omitted the weightier matters of the law, judgment, mercy, and faith; these ought ye to have done, and not to leave the other undone"* (Matthew 23: 23 KJV).

Instead of condemning tithing, he commends them for tithing even such items as garden herbs.

As children of Abraham, the father of the faithful, we are also heirs to the promises given to him by and through faith in Jesus Christ (Romans 4: 16; Galatians 3: 7).

Possibly a greater insight can be gained from Hebrews 6: 20 and 7; 11. Jesus, after His resurrection, was made a High

Priest after the order of Melchizedek. Levi, because he was yet in the loins of his father when his father met Melchizedek and paid tithes, paid tithes not because they were obligated under the law to do so, but because they were under grace.

Therefore, we, being the spiritual seed of Abraham and under grace, should pay tithes to Christ, the High Priest who is after the order of Melchizedek.

Because all scripture is given by inspiration of God and is profitable for doctrine, we can draw from the Old Testament, which is a shadow of things to come. The blessing of tithing is vividly expressed in Malachi 3: 10:

> Bring all the tithes into the store house that there may be meat in mine house, and prove me now herewith, saith the Lord of Hosts, if I will not open you the windows of heaven, and pur you out a blessing that there will not be room enough to receive it.

The purpose of tithing in the New Testament is to provide for God's ministers (1 Corinthians 9: 7-14, 1 Timothy 5: 17-18).

6

The Curse of Conscience

W e are familiar with the curse, which came upon mankind following Adam's sin:

> *Cursed is the ground for your sake; in toil you shall eat of it all the days of your life. Both thorns and thistles it shall bring forth for you, and you shall eat the herb of the field. In the sweat of your face you shall eat bread till you return to the ground, for out of it you were taken; for dust you are, and to dust you shall return (Genesis 3:17-19).*

We know that Christ has redeemed us from that curse, being made a curse for us (Galatians 3:13). But few may realize that despite Christ's sacrifice to redeem us, we can still perpetuate a curse upon ourselves from that day in the Garden.

Adam and Eve ate the forbidden fruit and in so doing became like God in their knowledge of good and evil:

> *"The man has become like one of us, to know good and evil" (Genesis 3:22).*

Man did not become divine or gain any of God's exclusive attributes or power, but he did gain autonomy based on his knowledge of good and evil. God's knowledge of good and evil is pure, because it's not corrupted or polluted by deception or evil within. Man's knowledge of good and evil is subject to the deception of his heart (Jeremiah 17:9).

Before partaking of the Tree of Knowledge of Good and Evil, Adam and Eve had no concept of evil and no concept of good. They could not make that distinction. They were dependent on God to tell them what was good and what was evil. They had no way of proving God's assessment, because they lacked an intuitive, internal awareness of either good or evil. Theirs was truly a state of innocence. They did not understand how precious that innocence was until they had lost it forever.

Ruled by Conscience

From the moment Adam and Eve consumed the forbidden fruit, man has been ruled by his conscience instead of simple obedience to God. Man has become like God in that he must make up his own mind based on personal judgment between good and evil. Man became self-determining, self-judging, and lord and judge of his own behavior, independent of God's sovereignty. Eating of the Tree of Knowledge of Good and Evil immediately made man aware of his own sin. He found himself guilty before God, but instead of being under God's lordship and God's solution, man was forced to either accuse or excuse himself (Romans 2:15) under the power of his own conscience.

When man accepted the accusation of his conscience, he found himself in an awkward position. He knew that he was in the wrong and that he was out of fellowship with the only

One who could put him right. This led to defeat and shame and that which we identify today as "guilt feelings." Accusation is not the work of God. It's the work of the devil, the one identified as the "accuser of the brethren" (Revelation 12:10). When our conscience accuses us, it is complying with the works of the devil.

When man decides to excuse and justify himself, he enters into the deceit of his own wicked heart. This drives him further into rebellion against God and into thoughts that exalt themselves above the knowledge of God (2 Corinthians 10:5).

God does not excuse sin. However, the devil seduces us into hiding our sin in the darkness of self-deception. Then when our conscience excuses us, we are actually complying with the works of the devil.

Self-justification, based upon man taking control of his conscience, is common in the lives of many people. They are quick to justify adultery, greed, jealousy, revenge, anger, frustration and so on. They accept and promote thoughts of their own acceptability or self-righteousness in spite of their sin.

True Guilt

Scripturally, guilt is not a feeling, but a state of being—it is our standing before God. We are either guilty or not guilty, whether we feel accused or excused. We can feel guilty and yet be counted righteous in the sight of God. Likewise, we can feel righteous and assured that all is well while standing guilty in God's sight. Whether we are in the pit of depression and despair because of our failure and shame, or arrogantly continuing in sin with cocksure ideas of our own innocence, our true standing with God is unchanged. We are either guilty or righteous, based on what God says, and not on what we persuade ourselves to believe.

We escape the sentence of judgment through Christ: *"There is therefore now no condemnation to those who are in Christ Jesus"* (Romans 8:1). God does not judge us, because He has given judgment into the hands of the Son. When we are saved through faith in Christ, we have passed from judgment (John 5:20-25).

Jesus reveals how far removed He is from accusation through His encounter with Mary Magdalene. She was brought before Him by a group of accusers who were then dispersed by Jesus' challenge that anyone among them without sin should cast the first stone. Once they left, Jesus asked Mary, *"Where are those accusers of yours? Has no one condemned you?"* Accusers are only interested in condemning, not in restoring to wholeness the person in the wrong. Jesus, the only one without any sin, was the only one fully qualified to cast the first stone. Yet, He said to her, *"Neither do I condemn you; go and sin no more"* (John 8:1-11).

Jesus is not the one who condemns. There is no condemnation to them who are in Christ Jesus (Romans 8:1).

Driven By Conscience

If we are under the condemnation of our conscience, we will be driven to attempt to earn restoration with God. Our conscience will tell us that we are guilty and must somehow get right with God. We may already have confessed our sins and no longer be guilty in God's sight.

Nevertheless, our conscience is not the "hot-line" to the throne of God. Our own awareness of good and evil is what compels us to seek God. To respond to the sense of guilt our conscience conveys to us, we may attempt to punish ourselves, deprive and berate ourselves, or similarly work to break free from feelings of guilt.

As Christians, we should enter into rest, because we have ceased from our own labors (Hebrews 4:7-10). We don't need to pay for our sins again and again, because Jesus has already done that for us. All we need to do is confess our sins and He is faithful and just to forgive us and cleanse us from all unrighteousness (1 John 1:9). Feelings of guilt and the accusations of our conscience have become invalid, so we can rest in God's forgiveness.

> As Christians, we should enter into rest, because we have ceased from our own labors.

The trap for many Christians is that even though they've claimed Christ's forgiveness and are in right standing with God, they've not yielded their life to the Lordship of Christ. For this reason they continue to live under the power of the conscience, accusing or excusing themselves.

Many Christians live under the power of guilt feelings, which create anxiety, fear and anger. They allow their consciences to dictate whether or not they are in right standing with God. Instead of trusting the Word of God and the truth that they are justified before Him, they keep relying on their consciences for confirmation about their standing. They even assume that their guilt feelings are sent from God, possibly as a means of guiding and directing their lives.

God does not manufacture or use guilt feelings against us. Guilt is a state of being. We are either under the condemnation of guilt before God, or we are forgiven. Guilt has nothing to do with feelings. What we commonly identify as guilt feelings are our responses to the accusations of our consciences. If we are afflicted by such accusations, we have not yielded ourselves to the Lordship of Christ. Instead, *we* retain lordship over our lives.

> The conscience makes us responsible for our own actions and makes us lords of our own choices.

The conscience makes us responsible for our own actions and makes us lords of our own choices. What is the correct way to deal with this? Once we have accepted Jesus Christ as our Lord and Savior, we must refuse to recognize the accusations and excuses generated by our consciences. We don't become the masters of our own consciences, but we submit our consciences to God. We cease judging ourselves, and submit ourselves back into that place of innocence which Adam and Eve once enjoyed with God. It's there that God alone is responsible for accounting to us guilt or innocence.

Paul revealed that he had come to such a place when he declared:

"I do not even judge myself. For I know nothing against myself yet I am not justified by this; but He who judges me is the Lord" (1 Corinthians 4:3-4).

Paul had a conscience just like we do, so why didn't he use it? Aren't our consciences God's gifts to show us when we are out of order?

No! Absolutely not!

The conscience is our own inner voice that judges our behavior, but there is only one who judges righteously and that is God (1 Peter 2:23). It's not God's intention that we live under subjection to the conscience. That is why eating of the Tree of Knowledge of Good and Evil was forbidden to Adam and Eve. We are to be controlled by the conviction of God's spirit and not by the condemnation of our conscience (John 16:7-8).

The Negative Effects of the Conscience

If we are under the power of the conscience, then we are in bondage to the power of fear. Adam said:

"I heard Your voice in the garden, and I was afraid because I was naked; and I hid myself" (Genesis 3:10).

Consciousness of our unworthiness causes us to be filled with fear, which is the first repercussion of self-judgment. People living with guilt feelings are under the power of fear. They are tormented by thoughts of being discovered and then judged or punished, being unworthy to gain anything out of life, or being relegated to the leftovers of life.

Under self-judgment, we are filled with shame and feel the compulsion to hide ourselves. We lose naturalness, confidence and innocence. Adam and Eve were ashamed of themselves, so they hid. They could no longer just be who they were, nor could they be transparent and natural with one another or with God. All of the confidence, ease, joy and naturalness of their existence was swept away in a moment.

> The conscience also brings us under the curse of toil and struggle.

The conscience also brings us under the curse of toil and struggle. God placed this curse on Adam, resulting in the natural fruit of the earth being withheld unless he labored to make it produce. All of the ready fruitfulness of the earth was locked, forcing man to struggle to obtain it. The blessing turned sour, and the ready productivity became laborious toil. Sadly, many people today exist under these effects of living by the conscience, severely limiting their fruitfulness and productivity. They live in fear, shame, and lack of fruitfulness.

The servant in the Parable of the Talents who received only one talent was gripped by fear. He said, *"I was afraid, and went and hid your talent in the ground"* (Matthew 25:25). This parable teaches us that fear binds up fruitfulness. We are unable to generate an increase when we are bound by fear. Instead of sowing and reaping, we practice burying and hiding, and don't employ God's laws of prosperity. The apostle John taught that fear brings with it the thought of punishment (1 John 4:17-18). Fear is linked to the condemnation of our conscience, working to inflict punishment upon us. What a trap!

> There is no need for us to be punished for our own sins or faults, since Jesus received that punishment for us.

The modern notion of guilt feelings is an internal punishment process resulting from being "accused" by our consciences. Instead of accepting that God is our judge and that we are not to judge ourselves, we not only judge ourselves but also punish ourselves for our failures and sins. People often mutter condemning words over themselves, such as "Oh, you stupid thing!" Or they may decide that they only deserve to sit at home feeling miserable. This is done in the vain attempt that somehow this punishment will alleviate the feelings of guilt.

Again, guilt is a standing before God. If we are guilty, then that's how God perceives us. Our guilt, then, must be dealt with by applying the blood of Jesus, for only by His blood can our conscience be cleansed (Hebrews 9:14). Once our sin is confessed and God's forgiveness applied, we are set free from guilt, and we stand in righteousness. There is no need for us to be punished for our own sins or faults, since Jesus received that punishment for us.

The Gentiles, those not under Christ's salvation, became a law unto themselves (Romans 2:14), putting them in charge of their own lives. Being a law unto yourself is total independence from God's Lordship.

The result of salvation through Christ must be submission to His Lordship, renouncing the hold of the conscience and the accusing or excusing of your own thoughts. God becomes your judge in the place of your conscience. Therefore, if God declares that you are righteous, accept that righteousness in spite of any accusation from your conscience. Likewise, if God convicts you of sin, then accept that conviction and repent, despite any excusing from your conscience. Thus, you cease being a law unto yourself and become submitted to the law of the Spirit of life in Christ Jesus. That is what sets you free from the law of sin and death (Romans 8:2).

The Conscience or the Throne

Chris spent some years under a minister who was committed to challenging sin in the lives of his congregation. On several occasions, Chris was challenged about certain sins in his life that the minister believed needed to be addressed. Because Chris was more inclined to accuse than excuse himself, he made it his policy to accept every accusation as being from God. He repented even if he could not see the evidence of the problem defined by the minister.

This process went on for several years, and Chris found it beneficial to be able to clear out several things he would otherwise have overlooked. But the day came when the minister called to discuss a problem of which Chris felt himself absolutely innocent. Chris patiently listened as the minister presented his case. He told the minister that he would pray about it. As soon as the minister left, Chris stood up, lifted his hands to heaven and committed the entire accusation to the Lord. For the first time, he sensed that he was not to rely on the accusations brought by others, but to listen to the convicting voice of the Holy Spirit. He placed the issue into the Lord's hands, declaring sincerely that if the Holy Spirit convicted him, he would repent. But until that occurred, he would consider the matter a nonevent.

This was a significant turning point in Chris's life, as he began to depend more on the leading of the Spirit and not on the voice of man or his own conscience. That supposed sin was soon forgotten. Over the years, though, many occasions of repentance and tears have come and gone as God, by His Spirit, has revealed the deep thoughts and intents of Chris's heart, which needed to be brought to the Lord for cleansing.

Conviction vs. Accusation

Conviction by the Holy Spirit is entirely different from the accusation of our conscience. Accusation causes us to flee in fear and to hide ourselves from God as Adam did in the Garden. Accusation also awakens fear and torment, and focuses on judgment and punishment.

However, conviction causes us to have godly sorrow, which draws us to God in repentance:

> *Now I rejoice, not that you were made sorry, but that your sorrow led to repentance. For you were made sorry in a godly manner, that you might suffer loss from us in nothing. For godly sorrow produces*

repentance leading to salvation, not to be regretted;
but the sorrow of the world produces death
(2 Corinthians 7:9-10).

Under conviction, we are grieved that we have come short of the glory of God, but we are not afraid. Our hearts mourn, and we thereby receive the blessing of Jesus.

"Blessed are those who mourn, for they shall be comforted" (Matthew 5:4).

We respond as David did when he was convicted through the prophet, Samuel, for his sin with Bathsheba. David ran to God for mercy, confessed his sin and found complete forgiveness (Psalm 51).

Accusation results in our hiding in fear, while conviction results in our confessing in faith. No wonder the devil wanted Adam to partake of the Tree of Knowledge of Good and Evil. It brought man under the curse of condemnation—not just God's condemnation for sin, but man's personal condemnation resulting from a life-style ruled by the conscience.

> Accusation results in our hiding in fear, while conviction results in our confessing in faith.

Jesus dealt with our sin and broke the Adamic curse. In Him we are forgiven, we have liberty, we are blessed with all spiritual blessings in heavenly places, and we are declared righteous. We are freed from the curse of laboring to create an increase. We can cease from our own labors and enter into the rest that God has prepared for us, and God will bless the work of our hands. However, if we've not put aside our consciences, then we're still under the rule of that curse and cannot enter into the abundance and provision that is rightfully ours.

The word "conscience" is not found as such in the Old Testament, although there are several words used that are synonymous in the New Testament. When Adam and Eve ate of the forbidden fruit, their eyes were opened. Their moral understanding was awakened by their violation of God's command. They then had the power to discern the difference between good and evil. The consequence was that they had become a law unto themselves. (See Romans 2: 14-15.) When conscience is violated, the consequence is that fear and shame are engendered. Innocence is lost, and guilt is contracted.

Before their eyes were opened, they were both *naked and not ashamed*. Their nakedness (*e'rom*) represented their true humanity, their authentic self. They had no moral or character defects. They had no feelings of shame, inferiority, or self condemnation. After their consciences were awakened to the *knowledge of good and evil*, their inner beauty was marred, and they felt disfigured inwardly.

Adam and Eve became governed by conscience rather than the revealed Word of God. Three times in the book of Judges, a reference is made to the fact that *there was no king in Israel, and every man did that which was right in his own eyes*. One of the reasons given for the initial failure of the children of Israel entering the land of Canaan was that every man did that which was right in his own eyes.

The importance of having a cleansed conscience is revealed in 1 John 3: 21:
> ... *And, beloved, if our consciences (our hearts) do not accuse us [if they do not make us feel guilty and condemn us], we have confidence (complete assurance and boldness) before God* ...(AMP).

To live by conscience alone is to become a law unto self. It stops us from entering our Canaan (peace and prosperity).

7

A Prosperous Soul

beautiful statement about prosperity is found in 3 John 2: "Beloved, I pray that you may prosper in all things and be in health, just as your soul prospers."

Here we see that the level of prosperity we enjoy is linked to the condition of our soul. We could summarize it in this way, "fruitfulness follows healing."

Unresolved issues from our past bring injury to our lives, and those injuries hold us back from the blessings God plans for us. We need to resolve any and all issues that remain from our pests by presenting them to Jesus. He is the Good Shepherd who is able to restore our souls (Psalm 23:3).

The Prodigal Son

The story of the prodigal son recorded in Luke 15:11-32 is a wonderful example of a person missing out on God's best because of past sin. This son had been indulgent and self-focused, lusting for freedom that his father didn't provide him at home. Before his father's death, he asked to be given his inheritance and then he traveled to a far country where he squandered all that he had on riotous living.

When the inheritance his father had built up for him was spent, the prodigal discovered that he had no true wealth within himself. He had spent his life enjoying a level of provision that he was unable to provide for himself. His father's wisdom and management had provided the blessings he took for granted and enjoyed so carelessly.

Finally, Scripture says, he "came to his senses." This reveals that sin is akin to insanity. Sin is a falsehood that can captivate deceived hearts. Once sin worked its course in the prodigal and proved itself to be the destroyer that the Scripture says it was, he came to his senses and realized there had always been ample provision in his father's house.

The prodigal also realized that he was now unworthy of those provisions, but decided to find a way to come under the covering or protection of that blessing. He would ask to be a servant of his father's instead of a son. By humbling himself, he became worthy of the grace his father was waiting to bestow upon him.

Remorseful Memories

The prodigal's remorseful memories pronounced him worthy of demotion. He felt it was only right that he be punished and become a servant rather than a son.

Many of us have memories of experiences for which we still feel a need to be punished. Peter carried remorse after denying Jesus. He had been so confident in his faithfulness, but after denying Jesus, he remembered His words and with bitter tears became filled with remorse (Matthew 26:75).

For many years, Joseph's brothers repressed the memory of betraying their brother and lying to their father. However, one day, a day of great destiny they stood before an Egyptian ruler who spoke words that awakened their remorseful memories. The man was their brother, Joseph, but they didn't recognize him. When the brothers were confronted with references to lying, a younger brother, and being put in a pit, they began to feel condemnation for this old sin (Genesis 42: 19-22).

Many mental breakdowns result from the condemnation of past sin and minds filled with remorseful memories. People feel the need to be punished and their emotions set out to accomplish it. They are overcome by depression, which is anger turned inward. People emotionally turn the gun on themselves.

> Many mental breakdowns result from the condemnation of past sin and minds filled with remorseful memories.

Bringing Hidden Things to the Light

God knows the things in our lives that hold us back, and He wants to bring them into the light of His Word and His presence. God wants to expose those hidden things of shame so that we can renounce them and be released from the bondage. We *"have renounced the hidden things of shame, not walking in craftiness nor handling the word of God deceitfully"* (2 Corinthians 4:2).

One of the ways God brings hidden things to the surface is through association. For Peter, it was the crowing of a rooster that brought conviction (Matthew 26:73-75). For the Israelites in Babylon, it was singing the songs of their homeland that brought remorseful feelings:

By the rivers of Babylon,
There we sat down, yea, we wept
When we remembered Zion.

We hung our harps
Upon the willows in the midst of it.
For there those who carried us away captive asked
of us a song,
And those who plundered us requested mirth,
Saying, "Sing us one of the songs of Zion!"
How shall we sing the LORD's *song?*
(Psalm 137:1-4)

Healing Brings Fruit and Freedom

God's plan is to bring about our healing because once we are healed we can be fruitful. This pattern is illustrated in the life of Joseph. By the time he was established in Egypt with a wife and an important career, he named his first child Manasseh because God had caused him to forget his past afflictions. When his second child was born, he was named Ephraim, because God had made him fruitful in the land (Genesis 41:51-52). Healing the memories of past afflictions came first, and then came the fruitfulness.

To further illustrate this principle, I'll share this personal experience:

A number of years ago, my oldest son, Kerry, realized that he enjoyed too much the drinking of several beers after work each day. The fact that he was looking forward to the beers on a regular basis began to disturb him. He feared that perhaps he was becoming addicted and possibly headed toward alcoholism. When he attempted to discontinue the habit, he found that he could not do it by an act of his will. The desire for the beer remained.

The fact of the matter was that Kerry's soul needed to be set free. I wondered why Kerry's willpower alone wasn't enough

86

to conquer this habit. After seeking the Lord, I realized that my own spoken words before Kerry's birth had wounded his spirit. This proverb was being lived out before my very eyes: *"A wholesome tongue is a tree of life, but perverseness therein is a breach in the spirit"* (Proverbs 15:4).

When Kerry was born, I wasn't ready to be a parent and wanted to wait a while longer before having children. When told of the untimely news, I unwittingly rejected my firstborn child by the words I spoke expressing my disappointment. Of course, after Kerry was born, I loved him very much, but the seed of rejection had been sown and pierced Kerry's tender, young spirit.

> God wants us to prosper, but He knows that our soul must prosper first.

When I confessed this, repented and accepted responsibility, Kerry was wonderfully delivered. The wound in his spirit was healed, therefore, his soul and body was set free.

God wants us to prosper, but He knows that our soul must prosper first. So, He endeavors to show us those areas in our lives that need restoration. The diligent seek out the truth and are set free. However, the selfish and willful resent and deny that they have problems and limitations to their prosperity. Therefore, they remain in an unprofitable state. Allow the Lord to open your eyes to see the work of restoration He wants to accomplish in your life so that you can submit to Him, become complete, and prosper in the Lord's purposes.

Breaking the Curse

Another area that restricts the soul is the issue of curses spoken over our lives. Our souls are not as robust as we think or desire them to be. Oppressions that come upon our lives impact our souls even though we are determined to believe in the strength of our minds and power of our souls.

> Everything that oppresses our souls will limit our prosperity.

I discovered an area of financial oppression that was limiting me when an event from the life of my grandfather came to light. Grandfather had owned a relatively large land holding in Australia when he received word that an inheritance was his to claim in England. It would be an extended journey, and he was going to be gone for quite some time.

To his sons' surprise, their father arrived back in only a matter of days. He had changed his mind about collecting the inheritance and declared to his sons: "What's the use of collecting the inheritance? You boys will only waste it."

Those words were a curse upon the lives of the sons. Furthermore, as a child of one of those sons, I realized this curse was at work in my own life as well. Through this revelation, the curse was prayed over and broken in the name of Jesus.

Everything that oppresses our souls will limit our prosperity. We need to make "soul prosperity" a matter of prayerful concern and priority, inviting the Holy Spirit to move upon our lives, revealing what is out of order so that the grace and glory of the love of God may transform us.

8

Dealing With Unfruitfulness

Many people follow Scriptural guidelines for their finances, but never reap a harvest from their sowing. They give, but do not receive. They do everything they know to be faithful to God, yet are constantly struggling.

The children of Israel experienced similar circumstances as are recorded throughout the Bible. One such occasion is found in Judges 6. The Midianites were oppressing Israel by stealing their harvest and destroying the seed they had sown.

Similarly, in the Parable of the Sower, we have a record of seed growing, but a failure to bear fruit (Mark 4:1). By studying Scripture, we discover that there are two ways we can be robbed of fruitfulness. Both of these circumstances are linked to the condition of our heart:

1. Influences and oppressions from the outside.
2. Conditions from within.

What You Worship

Several factors contribute to being unfruitful.

Factor #1: Conditions from without are caused by conditions from within.

In the case of Israel as recorded in Judges 6, the Midianites were allowed to oppress Israel, steal their productivity and spoil their fruit, because the nation was out of order. In fact, Israel was worshipping the gods of the Amorites in direct disobedience to God's instruction (Judges 6:10).

The people cried to the Lord, and in answer to their pleas, God raised up Gideon as a deliverer. However, for Israel to be free from the Midianites, Gideon was required to first lead an attack against the false worship. He was called by God to pull down his father's altar to Baal before God asked him to do anything more (Judges 6:25-26). If Gideon had failed to challenge the sin of idolatry, God would not have led him in victory over the Midianites.

The attack on the prosperity of Israel was from without, but was a direct result of the condition within the hearts of the people. They had disobeyed God and worshiped the false gods of those around them.

Israel was "oppressed by the people whose god we serve"— the Midianites. When we worship anything other than God Himself, the people wholly committed to that thing we worship become our oppressors. For instance, if Israel worshiped Baal, then the true worshipers of Baal oppressed them. However, if Israel worshiped the Lord God, the Midianites would not have been able to spoil their prosperity. The Midianites oppressed Israel because Israel worshiped the god of the Midianites. This propagated spiritual weakness and brought Israel under the physical oppression of the people to whom they were spiritually submitted.

Likewise today, if as God's people we worship:
- fame, those who worship fame oppress us.

- money, the worshipers of money oppress us.
- success, then the people who worship success oppress us.

The oppression comes from without, but the problem is from within. There is no reason to wonder why we are put down, humiliated, or intimidated, or why our plans are frustrated. The answer is simple. The people who disturb and unsettle us and who block and frustrate us have the power to do so as long as we worship the things they serve.

It is vital that we search our hearts to discover the things we long for and worship. When found, they must be renounced and we must commit ourselves to serve only the living God. Once we have renounced the worship of those "things," we are able to win back the ground lost to the enemy. Once we judge our own hearts and return wholeheartedly to the Lord, we will be delivered from the intimidation, destruction and the ravaging of our fruitfulness.

The issue cannot be avoided. Covetousness must be dealt with because it is idolatry:

"Therefore put to death your members which are on the earth: fornication, uncleanness, passion, evil desire, and covetousness, which is idolatry" (Colossians 3:5).

Jesus warned us:

"Take heed and beware of covetousness, for one's life does not consist in the abundance of the things he possesses" (Luke 12:15).

Factor #2: Cares of the world.
When we are absorbed in the cares of this world and fooled by the deceitfulness of riches, our fruit withers on the vine. Only two places where the seed was sown in the Parable of the Sower did it survive, but only one brought forth fruit (Mark 4:3-8). The seed that fell on the pathway and on thorny

ground lived. However, only the seed that fell into good ground brought forth fruit. The seed that fell among the thorns survived, but it was choked into unfruitfulness.

Note that nothing was wrong with the seed. The seed was good and productive, and the fruitfulness of the plant was not dependent on the seed itself. The seed was destined to be productive, but it depended upon the fertility of the soil into which it happened to fall.

You may be doing the right things scripturally—planting the right seed and following the right instructions—but receiving no fruit from your labors. Don't question the seed. Do a soil test on your heart instead. Search for the two things that make the soil unproductive:

"Now he who received seed among the thorns is he who hears the word, and the cares of this world and the deceitfulness of riches choke the word, and he becomes unfruitful" (Matthew 13:22).

What are the things that the world cares about? John lists the world's major focuses in 1 John 2:16: *"The lusts of the flesh, the lust of the eyes, and the pride of life."* The world wants you to care about pleasing yourself by looking good and feeling good in your own estimation. But God wants you to live for Him.

When you become immersed in the things of the world, you are choked by those cares and are powerless to bring forth fruit in God's kingdom. The world only cares about pleasing itself. Its mantra is, "If it feels good, do it." The advertising, marketing and merchandising of products and services is based on the expectation that people will seek to please themselves.

When you consider the money in your hands as an opportunity to please yourself, which is what you've been trained to think since your early childhood, you're already on course to be choked by the cares of this world.

Factor #3: The deceitfulness of riches.

The deceitfulness of riches is a succinct way to express the reality of the lie that money symbolizes. Most people are completely convinced that money will solve all their problems. They are consumed with the notion that if they have enough money, they'll be happy. However, this is total deception and vanity. This deception is so seductive that sincere Christians are happier with money in their pockets than the promises of God in their hearts. So this begs the question: Which is the greater: God or money?

Jesus taught that we couldn't serve two masters, God and mammon (money). This message cuts to the heart of those Christians totally consumed with the anticipation of getting ahead financially. Riches deceive them into thinking that it's a requirement for happiness and fulfillment. However, the pursuit of riches fosters a self-serving interest in money, and violates the truth that money is God's property placed in our possession for His purposes. Sadly, too many Christians take hold of money, believing that it will guarantee that which God may withhold.

Paul made a startling statement about the danger of being absorbed with money. He said that to be spiritually minded is life and peace, but to be carnally (or naturally) focused is death (Romans 8:6). When we serve God, we enjoy life and peace. When we succumb to the deceptive lure of riches, we pursue death. It's as simple as that.

What's in your heart?
- Do you worship and covet things?
- Are you caught up in the cares of this world?
- Are you under the power of the deceitfulness of riches?

If you honestly answer yes to any of these questions, you are being robbed of fruitfulness in one way or another.

Unfruitfulness: The Bottom Line

Unfruitfulness occurs in one of two ways. No matter which way it comes about, the bottom line is unfruitfulness, and your labor is in vain. You're either being robbed of the achievements of your productivity, or choked into unproductiveness.

There are countless ways that we can be robbed of fruitfulness, including:
- bad debts
- medical bills
- unwise investments
- poor advice
- unexpected charges
… the list goes on

These experiences are common and the "hole-in-the-pocket" problem is a universal experience.

Being choked by troubles, and being distracted and swamped by the issues of life generates a loss of fruitfulness. We may know what to do, fully intend to do it, and despair at the lack of our progress, but all the while we are hemmed in by circumstances, pressures, difficulties and distractions that prevent us from moving forward. This is the experience of seed sown among the thorns. The plant is potentially strong and fruitful, but it couldn't compete with the other plants. The available resources and space are consumed by the thorns and taken over by them.

Sometimes we lose our fruit because it's taken away, while on other occasions we're denied the opportunity to be fruitful. When we have cleansed our hearts and prepared the soil for the seed, we can rectify the unfruitfulness and enter into the productivity of the Lord.

The Devourer

We looked at the role of the devourer in the chapter on tithing. We learned that when we withhold the tithe from God, we are cursed with a curse and God allows the devourer to come into our circumstances. The devourer robs us of fruit, just as we have robbed God of the tithe.

> 'You are cursed with a curse, For you have robbed Me, Even this whole nation. Bring all the tithes into the storehouse, That there may be food in My house, And try Me now in this,' Says the LORD of hosts, 'If I will not open for you the windows of heaven And pour out for you such blessing that there will not be room enough to receive it. And I will rebuke the devourer for your sakes, So that he will not destroy the fruit of your ground, Nor shall the vine fail to bear fruit for you in the field,' Says the LORD of hosts (Malachi 3:9-11).

If you are wrestling with unfruitfulness, then be sure it's not the devourer with whom you are contending. If you are robbing God, then the devourer will rob you. The Lordship of God over your finances and over all of your life is the starting point for any expectation for blessing. If you compete with God for your money, you will be the loser.

Sadly, many people think they can provide for themselves. They set goals to achieve and are determined to reach them even if it isn't in God's plan for them. This is foolishness and like chasing the wind. The Psalmist makes it perfectly clear that unless we have God's blessing upon what we are doing, we are engaged in vanity. Don't forget we are not in control; God is:

> *"Unless the* LORD *builds the house, they labor in vain who build it; unless the* LORD *guards the city, the watchman stays awake in vain" (Psalm 127:1).*

– 9 –

Gain or Loss

The inclination to trust in riches and be ruled by covetousness is nowhere more obvious than in the issue of "gain or loss." The desire for gain and the fear of loss is a widely respected instinct that is often capitalized on by marketers and salespeople in our consumer society.

Christians are cautioned against submitting to the desire for gain or the fear of loss. We are admonished to trust God completely and implicitly in every situation. This is not an optional life-style reserved only for the extraordinarily devout, but is a clear teaching of Scripture that applies to all of God's people.

Take No Thought

Jesus said, *"Do not worry about tomorrow"* "(Matthew 6:34). If we are controlled by the desire for gain or the fear of loss, we'll be preoccupied with thoughts and worries about tomorrow. We will give thought to our provision and how to protect it. Jesus told us not to worry, saying *"Seek first the kingdom of God and His righteousness, and all these things shall be added to you"* (Matthew 6:33).

We know and understand these Scriptures and have no real problem with them until we attempt to become serious about following them. In practical terms, it appears absurd to live in our western culture without planning for, borrowing for, worrying about and giving thought to tomorrow. Yet this is precisely what Jesus is telling us to do.

> God has not assigned us to a life of poverty and deprivation, but to a life of faith and abundance in all things.

God didn't give us these instructions for the purpose of withholding good things from us, but that we may have His blessing in His way. God has not assigned us to a life of poverty and deprivation, but to a life of faith and abundance in all things.

The mentality of many Christians has been, "If we give in to God, we will go without." So they determine to achieve their own financial and life goals. They seek to appease God with an offering now and then or volunteer on occasion, but do not allow Him to interfere with their plans. Such attitudes are not covetous but based on a false understanding of God.

God delights in the prosperity of His servants (Psalm 35:27). He wishes above all things that you prosper and be in good health (3 John 2). God gives you the power to gain wealth (Deuteronomy 8:18), and is not trying to restrict, deprive or rob you. Covetousness and unbelief cause you to doubt and distrust the Lord. Covetousness causes you to interpret God's challenge to live by faith, have His values, and obey His daily guidance as an attack on your independence—a roadblock keeping you from the things after which your heart lusts. The desire for gain and the fear of loss perpetuate a false perception of God as the great depriver instead of the great provider.

Jesus' instruction not to worry about tomorrow is not meant to encourage an irresponsible attitude toward money and possessions. In fact, Jesus talked about first sitting down and counting the cost of building or going to war, properly evaluating the situation and then acting accordingly.

> *For which of you, intending to build a tower, does not sit down first and count the cost, whether he has enough to finish it—lest, after he has laid the foundation, and is not able to finish, all who see it begin to mock him, saying, 'This man began to build and was not able to finish.' Or what king, going to make war against another king, does not sit down first and consider whether he is able with ten thousand to meet him who comes against him with twenty thousand? Or else, while the other is still a great way off, he sends a delegation and asks conditions of peace (Luke 14:28-32).*

Jesus does not advocate a mindless, careless, blind attitude. We are expected to take serious stock of our situations, and be responsible and accountable. Even the passage quoted above finishes with a challenging statement:

> *"So likewise, whoever of you does not forsake all that he has cannot be My disciple" (Luke 14:33).*

Our attitudes toward gain and loss must be radically different from those of the culture in which we live. We must count God as our gain and have already given up everything for Him in order to be unaffected or drawn away by material possessions. Paul expresses this priceless heart attitude in Philippians 3:8, 14.

God Governs Our Gain and Loss

The issue of gain and loss is very clearly discussed in Psalm 127:1: *"Unless the Lord builds the house, they labor in vain who build it: Unless the Lord guards the city, the watchman stays awake in vain."*

No matter how determined you are to achieve gain and to create something in this world for yourself, God is able to completely frustrate your plans and progress. He is able to halt it altogether, or let you finish it before He pulls it down. If God is not releasing gain to you, then your desire to accumulate and establish something for yourself is useless.

> If God is not releasing gain to you, then your desire to accumulate and establish something for yourself is useless.

No matter how determined you are to protect and defend your kingdom against all possible encroachments, God is able to destroy it in an instant. Your security system, insurance policies, watchfulness and hired guards are no protection, and you're relying on a false assumption. If God has determined it's necessary to take away all you have built that is contrary to His will and motivated by wrong reasons, then there is nothing you can do to protect it.

Therefore, both gain and loss are under God's control. Nevertheless, most people in our culture are preoccupied with one or both of these concerns. People work longer hours and struggle through all manner of obstacles in desperate attempts to gain something for themselves. Others lock away their lives and possessions in a determined effort to keep moth, rust, inflation and deterioration from taking their tolls.

Sales people have learned how to use the desire for gain and the fear of loss as basic trigger mechanisms in selling. One strategy sales people use to compel us to buy is telling us that we have a limited time to make a decision or another buyer will beat us to the purchase. It's also quite normal for sales people to praise the virtues of a product until every desire to gain it and claim it as our own has been fully awakened. This is very manipulative use of basic, carnal motivation. But if we are shallow enough to be motivated by gain and loss, do we deserve anything better because of our wrong focus?

The Answer is Trust and Contentment

Trust is the only answer to a preoccupation with gain and the fear of loss. When we entrust our lives to God, we are able to take no thought for tomorrow and live a day at a time. We don't have to lose sleep visualizing what we want to gain or worrying about what we might lose. When we arrive at the place of trust, we find contentment in our "great gain," described in 1 Timothy 6:6.

This same passage gives us a sober warning against coveting money and gain:

> And having food and clothing, with these we shall be content. But those who desire to be rich fall into temptation and a snare, and into many foolish and harmful lusts which drown men in destruction and perdition. For the love of money is a root of all kinds of evil, for which some have strayed from the faith in their greediness, and pierced themselves through with many sorrows (1 Timothy 6:8-10).

This piercing through with many sorrows is reminiscent of the seed that landed among the thorns, which Jesus related to the deceitfulness of riches. When you believe the lie that money will make you happy—coveting gain and fearing loss—and especially the concern that God may frustrate your desires, you err from the faith and pierce yourself through with the thorns of sorrow.

The Christian's Alternative

Our true gain is the Lord. He is the *"fountain of living waters"* (Jeremiah 2:13), *"my rock and my fortress and my deliverer; my God, my strength, in whom I will trust; my shield and the horn of my salvation, my stronghold"* (Psalms 18:2). The world is gripped by the need to gain and protect. However, Christians have entered into a different realm of experience where we don't need to struggle for gain or fear loss. If someone comes to take something away from us, we should give more than they asked for (Matthew 5:41-42).

Additionally, we are not gripped by the desire to gain when we see something that we don't have. We know that God will supply all our needs, and we've learned to be content with what we have. We have nothing to gain by adding another trinket or asset to our collection. If our needs are met and we have contentment, what gain is there in adding another thing to our possessions?

Sadly, this simple and clear teaching of Scripture is generally ignored today. Often, we don't believe that God can be trusted, so we determine it's essential to make provision for ourselves. Once we lose trust in God, there is no other recourse but the drive of desire for gain and the fear of loss.

Our prayer is that your heart will hear what Abram heard in Genesis 15:1: *"Do not be afraid. I am your shield, your exceeding great reward."*

With that revelation, there is no need to enter into protective or accumulative behaviors. Our hearts and minds are at peace, and we have entered into the blessings of the Most High God.

10

Prosperous Poverty

.

If anything produces fear in the heart of a covetous person, it is the thought of being poor. Poverty is regarded in our western culture as the most terrible blight of humanity. We are so accustomed to having things and so set on enjoying them that poverty and lack of "things" is a very fearful condition indeed.

However with regard to prosperity, Jesus illustrated a revelation that overturns the covetous notions of our hearts. He taught that poverty can release a great blessing and revealed an entirely new reason for prosperity. But we'll not understand the truth Jesus revealed if we're locked into the covetous ideas of wealth dictated by our culture.

We presume that wealth is principally for our own benefit. We also suppose that wealth must be measurable to be appreciated. A covetous heart wants to quantify wealth and utilize it all to satisfy its lusts. But Jesus saw prosperity and possessions from a completely different perspective.

Jesus Became Poor

Before coming to earth, Jesus was fabulously wealthy beyond imagination. It is impossible for us to comprehend or appraise the wealth of God. Jesus owned the wealth because He is God. Yet He laid it all aside (every evidence and expression of it) to become human so that He could identify with and minister to us. His intentions were good—to bring to us salvation. We would then be able to possess everything He had given up.

> "For you know the grace of our Lord Jesus Christ, that though He was rich, yet for your sakes He became poor, that you through His poverty might become rich" (2 Corinthians 8:9).

Christ's poverty would probably have been all the more real to Him because He was well aware of what He left behind. Jesus took upon Himself a state of poverty in order to bring blessing to others. By relinquishing His wealth, Christ was able to use it in a most powerful way. Jesus did not use wealth for personal satisfaction, but turned it into a vehicle of ministry to bless our lives. The process was not what we would expect. We would conceive of an even distribution of His wealth or the establishment of a trust fund to disburse the treasure. But Jesus used quite a different process. He chose to lay it all down and become poor.

Jesus' Prosperous Poverty

The amazing result of this decision is that Jesus became prosperous in His poverty. He had nowhere to lay His head (Matthew 8:20), and He was not operating on a huge budget with the resources and support of a wealthy family. Jesus maintained His ministry from the humble provisions supplied along the way. He laid claim to nothing, amassed no wealth, and maintained no storehouse from which to draw.

Nevertheless, Jesus freely gave to others far more than the wealthiest would have been reluctant to provide. He lived in "prosperous poverty."

When the five thousand needed to be fed, Jesus provided enough food for the crowd (with five loaves of bread and two fish borrowed from a child), and when they were finished, collected twelve baskets full of leftovers. When Peter committed Jesus to pay tribute (taxes), the money was supplied from the mouth of a fish. Jesus dined at fabulous banquets and traveled by boat while others went on foot. When He needed a donkey or an upper room, they were made available to Him without charge or complication.

Jesus in His poverty lived as well as someone of means. Jesus lived as if He were wealthy, yet He had no visible wealth upon which to draw. He was poor by worldly standards, yet was rich beyond measure. Jesus proved His own words: *"one's life does not consist in the abundance of the things he possesses"* (Luke 12:15). He possessed nothing, but had access to everything. Jesus shunned wealth and laid aside what was His, taking upon Himself the form of a servant (Philippians 2:6-8).

> Jesus lived as if He were wealthy, yet He had no visible wealth upon which to draw.

Jesus wasn't working some deal with God that if He gave up enough He could get some more. There was no covetousness in Jesus toward money and possessions. He trusted God to keep His possessions until He returned to possess them. Jesus' motivation in coming to earth, becoming poor, taking upon Himself the form of a servant and being obedient unto death was for OUR BEST GOOD. His focus was on us and not on Himself, which is the opposite of covetousness.

Jesus loved God enough to do His will despite the personal cost. And He loved us enough to pay the price for our blessing. This is at the very heart of stewardship. Covetousness is totally self-centered and selfish. Our flesh lusts toward covetousness, while our spirit craves to serve God in faithful stewardship.

Giving Up Wealth for Others

True riches only come forth out of poverty. Jesus had to become poor so that we could become rich. Everything He gave up became something we could gain. Jesus left heaven so that we could go there, and He came to earth so we could be seated in heavenly places in Him (Ephesians 2:6). Jesus was bruised, whipped and scarred so that we could be made whole (1 Peter 2:24). He took the torment upon His heart and mind so that we could be kept in perfect peace (Isaiah 53:5). God turned His face from Jesus and forsook Him, so Jesus could turn His face toward us and receive us (Matthew 27:46, John 6:37).

> Giving up what we have is the key to releasing blessings to others.

The lesson involving wealth and possessions is this: Giving up what we have is the key to releasing blessings to others. Wealth is not created for our indulgence, but as the means by which great blessing can be created. Others do not benefit merely by receiving material goods that we give to them. But as we renounce covetousness and release the desire for possessions, we can choose to suffer disadvantage to open the flow of ministry from God to the needy. This "prosperous poverty" enables us to live with great supply as needed, but most significantly, it releases the stream of God's provision for those who have no means of their own.

True Wealth

One can be wealthy by the world's standards, but still feel empty and unsatisfied. It's possible to be surrounded by possessions, yet have no contentment or fulfillment. It's also possible to possess nothing, yet be truly rich. Jesus didn't have His own place to rest His head, but He was in no way a poor man. Jesus taught His disciples to give to the poor, and sent Judas out for that purpose from time to time. Jesus wasn't a poor man needing charity, but a man of means distributing to the needs of others. You don't need outward evidence of prosperity to be truly prosperous.

Paul knew how to abound and how to be abased and how to be content in either condition (Philippians 4:12). Yet Paul was consistently aware that God would supply all of his needs according to God's riches in glory by Christ Jesus (Philippians 4:19). Therefore, the outward evidence made no difference to Paul. He knew God blessed him. But most important, he wanted to be a blessing to others. Paul brought the great wealth of the gospel—the unsearchable riches of salvation—to those in darkness by dying to his own considerations of wealth and provision. Paul even turned down money from some of the churches, choosing to earn a living through his trade as a tent maker instead (2 Thessalonians 3:8). Paul was not in the ministry for personal gain, but for the benefit of others.

> You don't need outward evidence of prosperity to be truly prosperous.

This is the attitude of heart that generates prosperous poverty. It is a worldly poverty by choice. It is willfully turning away from visible means of support and measurable tokens of wealth to minister to the real poverty of soul in others. This is a poverty that comes after the deathblow to covetousness has been struck, releasing God's ability to devote your life to the eternal gain of others.

This prosperous poverty is centered in the fear of God and the understanding that the earth is the Lord's and all that is within it. *"The silver is Mine, and the gold is Mine, says the* Lord *of hosts"* (Haggai 2:8). *"All things were created through Him and for Him"* (Colossians 1:16).

Prosperous poverty is also the result of a changed value system that focuses the heart and mind on storing up eternal treasures in heaven.

> *"While we look not at the things which are seen, but at the things which are not seen: for the things which are seen are temporal; but the things which are not seen are eternal" (2 Corinthians 4:18).*

True poverty declares: "None of this is mine; it all belongs to God." The poverty that prospers comes with yielding the rights of ownership back to God. We may have it to use, but we don't own it. This is not just a matter of saying, "I give my business to the Lord." It's a real commitment made with true humility, which is the correct attitude toward the right of ownership.

Prosperous poverty also involves proper motives. Much of the "prosperity doctrine" taught today appeals to people's lusts and covetousness. People send their money and commit themselves to giving schemes hoping to attract God's attention because they covet a blessing. However, the motivation of prosperous poverty is a desire to bless others at your own expense, not to seek a blessing through your acts of devotion and piety.

We cannot arrive at this place until we have put to death all covetousness in our lives (Colossians 3:5). Covetousness is idolatry, and idolatry is claiming things for your own. By claiming things and clinging to them, you exalt the created things above the Creator.

The Case of Nebuchadnezzar

A classic case of learning humility is seen in the life of the Babylonian King Nebuchadnezzar. He was an arrogant man who demanded that people worship him. He constructed a huge golden image and decreed that people bow down before it and worship or be thrown into a fiery furnace (Daniel 3:1, 4-5).

When Shadrach, Meshach and Abed-Nego refused to bow down to worship the idol, they were thrown into the furnace. But to the great astonishment of everyone, they walked about in the fire instead of burning. When Nebuchadnezzar looked into the furnace, he saw not three but four men in the fire, and the fourth man was "like unto the Son of God" (Daniel 3:25). King Nebuchadnezzar was amazed and so deeply impressed that he rescinded his demand that the people worship his image. Instead, he decreed that anyone speaking evil of the God of Shadrach, Meshach and Abed-Nego should be cut into pieces (Daniel 3:29).

Despite all this new insight, the king still considered himself the possessor of great power on the earth. His heart was not yet humbled. Though he recognized the true God, Nebuchadnezzar had not recognized his own humble state before an Almighty God. He thought he was the one with the power and thus had the right to command the people to worship this miracle-working God.

Nebuchadnezzar, in this haughtiness and pride, was quite accustomed to making decrees. The lives of men and women hung in the balance on his proclamations. Though he acknowledged God and was impressed by God's power, he still thought of himself as the "great potentate." He even went so far as to make a decree in defense of the great God.

However, God set about to humble Nebuchadnezzar's heart. God did this by making His own decree that this great king was powerless to resist—a decree that would humiliate this raging potentate and turn him into a mindless fool.

> **We will never know the blessing of true riches until we release our possessiveness of wealth.**

One year after God's warning, Nebuchadnezzar was walking in his palace boasting about the great kingdom he had made for himself. He said, *"I have built"* all of this (Dan. 4:30). While the words of pride and arrogance were in the king's mouth, a voice from heaven said, *"The kingdom has departed from you"* (Dan. 4:31). Immediately, Nebuchadnezzar lost his reasoning power, and he lived in the fields like a wild animal for the next seven years.

At the appointed time, Nebuchadnezzar's reason returned to him, and he immediately began to praise God. He was now poor in spirit. He didn't consider himself as owning anything, but saw wealth and possessions as expressions of God's grace. He now knew that God alone had power over the affairs of men. He blessed, praised and honored God as the One who lives forever and whose dominion is everlasting from generation to generation (Dan. 4:34-37).

Until God humbled him, Nebuchadnezzar had held tightly the things he possessed as if they were his own. By holding onto his possessions, he endangered his own welfare and put himself into a place of great humiliation. Once he released the things in his possession and realized that everything belonged to God, he achieved humility, or poverty of spirit, which made him truly rich.

We will never know the blessing of true riches until we release our possessiveness of wealth. We must understand that all things belong to God and that He gives to whom He wills. Once we have achieved meekness and a place of true poverty, we are able to enter into the prosperous poverty evidenced in the life of Jesus.

Abram learned the secret of possessing abundance. When Melchizedek, the King of Salem, served Abram the bread and wine (which represented the body and blood of Christ), he gave Abram the revelation that God is the Most High Possessor and Maker of heaven and earth.

When the King of Sodom offered Abram the recovered spoil of Sodom, Abram refused, saying:
> *"I have lifted up my hand unto the Lord, the Most High Possessor of heaven and earth" (Genesis 14: 22).*

This statement and act signify that he yielded right of ownership of all to the Lord. This is true humility of heart, which is the gateway to abundant prosperity. Later in scripture, we read the testimony of Eliezer concerning God's goodness toward Abraham:
> *"And the Lord has blessed my master mightily, and has given him flocks, herds, silver, gold, menservants, maidservants, camels and asses" (Genesis 24: 35).*

True humility (lowliness of mind) is to esteem another more highly than oneself.
> *Let each one of you esteem and look upon and be concerned with not [merely] his own interests, but also the interests of others (Philippians 2: 3-4 AMP).*

We are encouraged to have this same attitude of mind as was in Jesus Christ Himself, who made Himself of no reputation in order to become a servant to all (Philippians 2: 7-8).

We see this humble attitude of mind in Abraham. When a conflict arose between the servants of Abraham and Lot, they had to separate. Abraham said to Lot:

> *"Is not the whole land before you? Separate yourself,*
> *I beg of you, from me. If you take the left hand, I will*
> *go to the right" (Genesis 13:9).*

Abram esteemed Lot's need as greater than his own.
> *As a reward for his humility, the Lord said to Abram:*
> *"Lift up you eyes and look from the place where you*
> *are, northward, southward, eastward, and westward.*
> *For all the land which you see I will give to you and*
> *your posterity, forever" (Genesis 13: 14-15).*

This is becoming poor in order to possess all things.

It is interesting to note that this same attitude that Abram
had is found in the early disciples in Jerusalem.
> *... And not one of them claimed that anything they*
> *possessed was [exclusively] his own, but everything*
> *they had was in common and for the use of all (Acts*
> *4: 32b, AMP).*

We must not confuse the word "common" with "communism,"
where the state owns all, but because we are joint heirs
together with Christ and His wealth, we are able to share
our abundance with those who lack the basic necessities of
life. This brings us to a coequality regarding finances to meet
out basic needs. The Apostle Paul emphasizes this truth in 2
Corinthians 8:13-14 where he encourages the Church to:
> *For it is not [intended] that other people be eased and*
> *relieved [of their responsibility] and you be burdened*
> *and suffer [unfairly]. But to have equality [share and*
> *share alike], your surplus over necessity at the present*
> *time going to meet their want and to equalize the*
> *difference created by it, so that [at some other time]*
> *their surplus in turn may be given to supply your want.*
> *Thus there may be equality ... (AMP).*

11

Prospering in Financial Famine

I s it possible to have a source of provision that is not affected by our natural circumstances? Is it possible to be well provided for at a time of recession or financial hardship? The biblical answer is a definite "yes." Philippians 4:19 says: *"My God shall supply all your needs according to his riches by Christ Jesus."* The supply is not according to the natural circumstances around us. Neither is it in the state of the economy, but *"according to God's riches in glory by Christ Jesus."*

How do we measure God's riches? How much does God possess in heaven? With streets paved in gold, there is unlimited wealth. The means by which we access these riches is "by Christ Jesus" or "in Christ Jesus."

We are in the position to access God's riches in glory by salvation accomplished through the sacrifice of Jesus. Jesus came to earth, willingly giving up physical health as He was whipped and crucified, so that by his stripes, *"you were healed"* (1 Peter 2:24).

Everything Jesus relinquished is made available to us. Furthermore, by belonging to Jesus and being a part of Him, we become heirs of God and joint heirs with Christ (Romans 8:17). We are inheritors of all of God's glory, and have access to God's riches in glory by Christ Jesus.

Dramatic examples exist of people receiving God's supernatural supply regardless of their natural circumstances:
- Ravens fed the prophet, Elijah (1 Kings 17:1-6).
- A widow's jar of oil that never ran empty (1 Kings 17:16).
- Five thousand people miraculously fed by Jesus (Matthew 14:20).
- Angels ministered to Jesus after His forty-day fast in the wilderness (Matthew 4:11).
- An angel gave Elijah heavenly food to sustain him for a long journey (1 Kings 19:5-8).
- Peter found a coin in a fish's mouth to pay taxes (Matthew 17:27).
- God supplied manna and quail in the wilderness for the nation of Israel (Exodus 16:13-15).

How are we to access this miracle supply when the circumstances around us are difficult? This is part of the prosperous poverty we discussed in the previous chapter. We must first acknowledge that God is the possessor of all things, and then live in daily obedience to Him.

The Example of Isaac

Isaac found himself in a famine and was unsure about what to do (Genesis 26:1-12). God spoke to him and told him not to follow his natural inclinations, but to follow the Lord's leading. Isaac was told not to go down to Egypt, which is what his father, Abraham, had done during the famine of his time. Isaac was not to follow the example of his forebears, but be ready to do a new thing. He was to obey the voice of God in fresh revelation, and not allow past experience to become a religious pattern for his life. God was not only the God of Abraham, but also the God of Isaac. Isaac had to make that a reality in his own life by waiting on God's fresh revelation and leading for his generation.

God told Isaac to dwell in a land which He would describe, and then said, *"Sojourn in this land, and I will be with you and will bless you"* (Genesis 26:3). Later in the same chapter, we see the fruit of that obedience, *"Then Isaac sowed in that land, and reaped in the same year a hundredfold; and the Lord blessed him"* (Genesis 26:12). Isaac received a hundredfold increase during a time of famine! Circumstances declared that it wasn't a time for good returns, yet Isaac prospered. And be sure, this was not the product of his scientific knowledge, agricultural skills or good management, although he was probably well equipped in all those areas. Isaac's success was a product of God blessing his obedience.

Isaac accessed the blessing of God by hearing and following God's voice. He had to put aside his natural tendencies and come into alignment with God's plan and purpose. How many of us today act by pure instinct or react out of fear of loss or the desire for gain? God looks at our individual situations differently and from a better perspective.

The Place to Sow for a Harvest

Jesus has presented us with a fertile land into which to sow for a great harvest. He has also revealed the best type of seed to sow for the finest results. In the Parable of the Sower, Jesus disclosed that the heart is the place to sow, and the thing to sow is the Word of God (Luke 8:4-15).

The amount of return is described in Matthew 13:23 as, *"some a hundredfold, some sixty, some thirty."* Imagine being able to get a thirty-fold return in bad times! Isaac scored a hundredfold return. How do we find such productivity and increase that is protected in hard times? We sow the WORD OF GOD into our HEARTS.

> By sowing God's Word into our hearts, we will have GOOD SUCCESS— the kind of success that brings only good to us.

Romans 10:6-10 declares that we should not allow doubt or questioning into our heart, but instead confidently believe that God has raised Christ from the dead. If we believe this, we will receive salvation. The Greek word *sozo* (translated "save") means to deliver, protect, heal, preserve, save, do well, be whole and make whole. Therefore, when we understand the fullness of the Greek meaning, all the provision and prosperity for which we could ever hope is included.

Joshua was instructed by God to keep God's words in his mouth and to meditate upon them. Then he would have "good success" (Joshua 1:8). Note that some people have the appearance of success, but it doesn't bring them good or happiness. They collect possessions or secure business breaks, but the consequences of success may be a broken home, a ruined life, a hollow personality, or a similar, miserable outcome. By sowing God's Word into our hearts, we will have GOOD SUCCESS—the kind of success that brings only good to us.

"The blessing of the LORD *makes one rich, and He adds no sorrow with it"* (Proverbs 10:22). This is the only kind of blessing worth having.

Psalm 1:2-3 describes the man who delights in the law of the Lord and who meditates in it day and night:

> But his delight is in the law of the LORD, And in His law he meditates day and night. He shall be like a tree Planted by the rivers of water, That brings forth its fruit in its season, Whose leaf also shall not wither; And whatever he does shall prosper.

Jeremiah 17:7-8 says something very similar, confirming the ability to be fruitful in difficult circumstances:

> Blessed is the man who trusts in the LORD, And whose hope is the LORD. For he shall be like a tree planted by the waters, Which spreads out its roots by the river, And will not fear when heat comes; But its leaf will be green, And will not be anxious in the year of drought, Nor will cease from yielding fruit.

Psalm 19:7-9 declares:

> The law of the LORD is perfect, converting the soul; The testimony of the LORD is sure, making wise the simple; The statutes of the LORD are right, rejoicing the heart; The commandment of the LORD is pure, enlightening the eyes; The fear of the LORD is clean, enduring forever; The judgments of the LORD are true and righteous altogether.

Notice that reference is made to the testimony of the Lord, the statues of the Lord, the commandment of the Lord, the fear of the Lord and the judgments of the Lord. This all-encompassing description in Scripture is associated with blessing. "And in keeping of them there is great reward" (v. 11).

John wrote that our material and physical prosperity is linked to the prosperity of our soul (3 John 2). Psalm 19:7 says that the Word of God converts or restores the soul, and Psalm 23:3 says that the good shepherd restores our soul.

117

Biblical Meditation

Scripture describes the process of planting God's Word in our hearts as meditating:

> *This book of the law shall not depart from your mouth, but you shall meditate in it day and night, that you may observe to do according to all that is written in it (Joshua 1:8).*

> *But his delight is in the law of THE LORD, and in His law he meditates day and night (Psalm 1:2).*

The two Old Testament words translated "meditate" mean "to mutter or to utter aloud." Therefore, this is not a reference to Eastern mysticism or the mindless meditation so popular in recent times. This is a reflection on God's Word involving the quiet speaking aloud of that Word. It even suggests speaking the Word out loud in surprise at the revelation brought to your spirit. Remember that faith comes by hearing the Word of God, and it is the Word of God that transforms us and renews our mind.

Another way of describing scriptural meditation is "chewing the cud"—the productive going over God's Word again and again. This allows it to be digested and engrafted by your inner man.

The Heart, Not the Head

A word of caution is necessary to make a clear distinction between sowing the Word in our hearts and sowing it in our heads. Psalm 119:11 says: *"Your word I have hidden in my heart, that I might not sin against you."*

The Word is supposed to be sown and hidden in our **HEARTS,** not in our intellects. Romans 10:9-10 speaks of believing in our **HEARTS,** which is different from having an intellectual understanding with our minds.

Seduction by the intellect has caused us to betray our faith. We seek understanding, knowledge and logical analysis, while God asks for belief from the heart. We assume that if our minds are satisfied, our hearts will follow suit. This assumption elevates the intellect to a place of honor, which is not taught or acknowledged in Scripture. God's Word admonishes us to fix our focus on attitude of heart and not on mental rationale.

The seed must be planted in our hearts. Fruitfulness is the result of sowing seed in a heart that is right before God. Sadly, many people have diligently studied the Word but still gain no benefit. They've sown the Word into their minds, but have not hidden it in their hearts. Being able to make this distinction is vitally important to your Christian life.

Integrating the Living Word into our Hearts

Material prosperity from a scriptural perspective is linked to prosperity of soul. Prosperity of soul is closely related to our intimacy with the Lord Jesus Christ, through our obedience to His Word and our faith and trust in Him regardless of our outward circumstances. To be content in any and every situation and maintain our peace comes only by becoming self sufficient in Christ's sufficiency (Philippians 4:13, AMP).

To achieve the kind of peace that passes all understanding— in order that we be anxious for nothing—only comes when we understand how to engraft the Word into our hearts (James 1: 21). The implanting of the Word contains the power to restore our souls.

The process of renewing the mind is achieved by biblical meditation. After our conversion to Christ, there will be conflicting thoughts and emotions that will affect our decisions. The flesh, our lower nature with tis passions and desires, must be brought under subjection to our reborn spirit. The inner conflict will paralyze the soul. As a result, we will suffer from boredom and lack of motivation.

The soul's response to this inner conflict will be:
• MIND: "I don't know what to do."
• EMOTIONS: "I can't take this anymore."
• WILL: "I don't know what to do."

Because the natural man's thoughts are contrary to God's thoughts (Isaiah 55: 3-9), one must cast down vain imaginations and strongholds of the mind (2 Corinthians 10: 4-5) that are contrary to the principles of God and expand on's human thoughts to God's thought. The mind is renewed by biblical meditation: the memorization and mastication of selected passages of scripture.

RENEWING THE MIND = Memorization + Mastication

REFOCUSING THE EMOTIONS = Personalization of scripture memorized + Harmonization

REFOCUSING THE WILL = Visualization of God's thoughts + Obedience to God's Word

As one begins to meditate on the Word, one's heart bears witness to the confession of the mouth. The agreement between the heart and the mouth will enable one to speak the word of faith (Romans 10: 4-5).

– 12 –

Heads – You Win!

We have not covered all that Scripture says about wealth, possessions and prosperity. Nevertheless, we trust that seeds have been sown into your heart that will produce abundant fruit for the kingdom of God. Our heart's desire is that you walk with the Lord, have a right heart before Him, be established in His Word and will be led by the precious Spirit of God.

Your greatest enemy in walking righteously before the Lord is your flesh. Beware of those who encourage your fleshly desires. They may present Scripture or other arguments to encourage you to covet this world's goods, but determine now in your heart to be done with covetousness forever.

If you have prayed through the issues raised in this book, you will most likely have a new and growing awareness of that which is righteous and that which is covetous. However, that may cause you to be more sensitive to the wrong attitudes than you were in the past. BE CAREFUL to not fall into the trap of being judgmental. Remember that the measure you use to judge others is the one God will use on you.

Purpose in your heart to forgive, love and pray for those whom you see caught in the snare of covetousness, lust and greed.

The doctrine of prosperity is probably one of the trickiest areas for Christians. It is true that the Lord delights in the prosperity of His servants (Psalm 35:27), but that never has been and never will be a license for us to seek prosperity. The popular concept is that because God wants us to be blessed, we should also want blessings for ourselves. But immediately our focus turns from the God we worship to the possessions we might acquire. We idolize the created things instead of worshipping the Creator.

Heads and Tails

The right attitude toward prosperity and God's blessing may be more easily understood by separating the one who imparts the value from the value assigned. Consider a coin with two sides: head and tail.

The head of the coin customarily depicts the current ruler and details of his authority to endorse the coin. The flip side, or tail side of the coin, usually contains a statement of the coin's monetary value. A coin usually has value as currency only in the country from which it originates. If another deposes the ruler of the land, there is no guarantee that the value on the flip side of the coin will continue to be honored.

During World War II, the Japanese, in preparation for their invasion and occupation of Australia, minted currency for use there. The currency carried the imprimatur of the emperor, conferring his endorsement to its value. It also had a value marked on the back. However, that currency never became legal tender because the Japanese army never occupied

Australia. During the war and in the years following, the only legal tender was currency minted in Australia that had the imprint of the Queen of England on the head and the Australian value on the tail. The Japanese money would only have had value if they had conquered Australia, which didn't happen.

Anyone can produce coins, but only the one who is truly in authority can endorse legal tender and make it worth anything. So it is with everything of value on the earth. We can admire all the trinkets and treasures this world offers, but never forget that they have no real value unless endorsed by the true head of the realm. The earth and the fullness thereof are the Lord's. So all of this world's wealth belongs to God. The coinage of the world, be it wealth, comfort, security, material resources or whatever, has value only if its "head side" comes from the living Lord God.

> So all of this world's wealth belongs to God.

Defacing the Head

Once the head side of a coin has been defaced, its value is lost. A coin will cease to be legal tender if it has been tampered with, especially if any attempt has been made to erase or deface the inscription of the ruler who authorizes its value. So it is with God's headship over the earth. If we deface the image of God or tamper with the coinage of the Kingdom, it ceases to have any value for us. When we hold the Head in esteem and properly honor Him, the value stamped on the tail side is endorsed.

Tragically, many people undertake to possess the things of this world and put their own imprimatur on them. They take the credit for building their wealth and value. People today are encouraged to pursue a course to prosperity instilled in them by our society and culture. The course may include study, degrees, qualifications, experience and climbing the corporate ladder, but it leads people to believe that they are the sources of their own success. People lose sight of the fact that God is the One who imparts value, and God gives us the ability to accumulate wealth.

Are They Satisfied?

It seems shallow to talk about owning things and yet not finding satisfaction in life. "Surely," our flesh tells us, "if I had the things I want, then nothing else would matter." But it does. The riches are only of value if they satisfy. Why else do we crave them? We expect them to minister something to us. We have faith in them. We trust them to make us feel good, and to give us power that will be somehow fulfilling.

We've already discussed this thinking under the heading "Deceitfulness of Riches." Our flesh is sold on the idea that riches will do wonderful things for us. Sadly, Christians are often happier with money in the bank than with the promises of God in their hearts. We ascribe great power and value to "things." It's possible and in fact very common, for many people to spend their lives and energies amassing wealth to satisfy their emptiness, only to discover that the expected satisfaction doesn't exist. Solomon recognized this as vanity— chasing the wind.

The bottom line is satisfaction. Once we've dealt a deathblow to the deception of money and set ourselves on a course to please and live for the Lord, we satisfy the great longing for comfort that others seek in the things of this world. They feel sorry for us because from their point of view, we are missing out on the possessions and fulfillment that they will undoubtedly acquire from achieving material gain. But the reality is that we are the ones achieving satisfaction and fulfillment. We know contentment. We've already arrived at the goal for which they are breaking their necks and selling their souls to attain. And, sadly, they won't ever arrive at that place of satisfaction, because they're looking in the wrong places.

The value of the world's entire economic system is dependent upon the endorsement of the ruler of the realm. Once you remove his image from the coin, it ceases to have value. It can't be spent, and it can't bring satisfaction to the purchaser. No matter how many coins you collect, they are worthless trinkets. People who refuse to honor the Lordship and Headship of God cannot find value and satisfaction from the coinage He created. The matter of Headship is vital in ratifying the value on the tail.

Heads – You Win!

This chapter has been entitled "Heads – You Win," because it's only when you give full and proper honor to the Lord as your King that you can expect to find value in anything else. You don't arrive at value by gazing at the tail-side of the coin and worshipping the value inscribed there. You must focus on the head side and give due worship and veneration to the One who provides the value in the first place.

Covetousness turns our attention to the tail side of the coin. Distrust of God turns our attention to the tail side. Self-interest turns our attention to the tail side. But all the while, if we look at the visible representation of the value, we miss the chance to truly possess and appreciate it.

God wants us to turn our attention to His image and superscription. He wants us to honor and worship Him

> *until we find that the tail side of the coin ceases to be*
> *of any interest. We aren't focused on things, goods,*
> *possessions, success or anything else. His honor and*
> *glory are all that have value for us. Then we can enjoy*
> *the true riches. Then the things that we have, whatever*
> *they may be, achieve their real value, and satisfy us.*
> *Then we will be truly satisfied for the first time:*
> *Ho! Everyone who thirsts, Come to the waters; And*
> *you who have no money, Come, buy and eat. Yes,*
> *come, buy wine and milk Without money and without*
> *price. Why do you spend money for what is not bread,*
> *And your wages for what does not satisfy? Listen*
> *carefully to Me, and eat what is good, And let your*
> *soul delight itself in abundance (Isaiah 55:1-2).*

The expression "Heads, you win!" comes from flipping a coin and relying on luck to decide an outcome. Luck is not involved in the real world of prospering in God's Kingdom. If you honor God as the "Head," you win. If you focus on the tail side—all the things you want—you lose. Where is your attention focused: heads or tails?

If we have achieved anything in this book, we pray that it serves to turn your attention from the things of this world—the prosperity you have sought, the gain for which you have longed, and the material items you have coveted—to a full and determined gaze into the Lord's face.

We want you to see Him in a new way. We want you to see Him as the giver and the source of all blessings. But in seeing Him as such, we don't want you to look into His hands to see what He may have for you and what you can convince Him to give you. We want you to be lost in the rapture of beholding His face and honoring Him. We want you to love and adore Him and to find your satisfaction in His presence. Then you will have resolved the issue of wealth and possession. You will possess everything, but hold on to nothing. You will have found your exceeding great reward.

My prayer is that the Lord blesses you richly as you find Him to be your all in all.